Corky Carroll – Not Done Yet

NOT DONE YET

The Autobiography

of the Legendary

Corky Carroll

Cover Art by Hans Backlund

Copyright © 2019 Corky Carroll All rights reserved.

No part of this book may be reproduced without the express written consent from the author, publisher or copyright holders. Except for a reviewer, who may quote brief passages in a review or promotion. Nor may any part of the contents of this book be reproduced, stored in a retrieval system, or transmitted in any form or by any means electronic, mechanical, photocopying, recording, or other means without the express written consent of the author, publisher, copyright holders or their assignees.

All photographs are the copyright of the credited photographer. In the event no credit is listed, the above paragraph applies.

The entire contents of this book are licensed and allowed for your personal enjoyment only. No part of this book may be re-sold or given away to others. If you would like to share this book or any part thereof, please purchase an additional copy for each person you would like to share with.

Cover design, editing & interior layout by The Productivity Group.

Version: 2020.03.23.3.b/w

ISBN: 978-0-578-62471-6

Corky Carroll – Not Done Yet

A huge THANKS to some of the people who helped me put all of this together and/or are a big part of the story.

All the members of my family and especially Raquel, Clint, Kasey, Tanner and Cannon. Who are my daily reminders of all things good in the world.

Doug "Duke" Parker
John Grannis and the Grannis family.
Tim Dorsey
John Severson
Doug Miller
Hobie Alter
Mickey Munoz
Mike Doyle
Steve Pezman
Joel Saltzman
Chris Rice
Ron Chrislip
Bill Yerkes
John Ford
Chris Darrow
Cheryl Carroll
Sarah Jacobs
Billy Hamilton
Des "Blue Dog" Metcalf
Mark Martinson
The Tashjian Family

AND... every person named, plus... a zillion others, who would take a whole nother book to list.

You know who you are.

Corky Carroll – Not Done Yet

Table of Contents

Page	Chapter	Title
4		Prelude
6	1	"First Ride"
12	2	"The Stoke"
17	3	"I'm Gonna be Good and… I Don't Care What You Think"
25	4	"Competition and Pre-Pro Years"
43	5	"The Turning Point"
57	6	"Turning Pro"
61	7	The Summer of… "The Endless Summer"
77	8	"The Brave New World"
88	9	"The Beginning of the Big Change"
95	10	"The Evolution"
110	11	"Prime Time"
117	12	"Peaking"
146	13	"The Mountains"
155	14	"Finding the Beat"
161	15	"SURFER Magazine"
167	16	"The Great Disaster"
169	17	"Tennis and Beer"
181	18	"Surfwear and Buckwheat"
190	19	"Tennis and Cars"
196	20	"Huntington Beach"
203	21	"Not A Good Wipeout"
213	22	"The Distant Sound of Mariachis"
221	23	"Mexican Time"
224	24	"Corkarita Time"
240	25	"A Learning Rebound"
246	26	"Finally Happy and Out to Pasture… Where I Belong!!!"
248		Epilogue
256		Epilogue II

My name is Corky Carroll and… I'm a Surfer!

PRELUDE

My parents loved me very much. This was obvious to me and everybody else who knew me as a child or when I was growing up.

I was born on September 29, 1947 – as Charles Curtis Carroll in Alhambra, California, a suburb of Los Angeles.

My dad was Charles Chester Carroll, carrying on a long line of Charles Carrolls. He was an electrician and my mom, Nellie, was a homemaker who had been a singer when she was younger.

When I was really little I had the colic and would make these little burping sounds all the time. Our neighbor had a dog that barked all the time and, from what I hear, it was hard to tell the difference between my burping sounds and the dogs barking. His name was Corky. So, you guessed it, they nicknamed me Corky after the neighbors barking dog.

I have never gone by anything else and probably would not respond if called by Charles. But call me Corky and I will come, fetch, roll over, shake hands and pretty much any other trick in the manual.

Although we lived in a nice neighborhood it was their feeling that this was not a great place to raise a kid.

Even then there was gang activity and the atmosphere was not really optimum for a peaceful and happy childhood.

So, when I was ready to start school, they decided to move us to the beach, and it was the best thing they ever could have done for me. Who even knows what would have become of me if we had stayed in the city.

One thing is absolutely certain though; my life would have unrolled much differently.

A Timeless Classic of Corky at Pipe – 1969
Photo: John Severson

CHAPTER ONE

"First Ride" ~ *7 years old*

Surfside Colony is a tiny strip of Southern California beach, just south of Seal Beach, which was lined with a few dozen weathered and battered wooden beach houses back in the 1950's. They were one step above what you could call "shacks" really. Our first house was a tiny one-bedroom affair with a little loft, which was where I slept.

The sound of the surf, which pounded in constantly, literally within' feet of our front door and the little window above my bed, pretty much drowned out everything else. It became the soothing lullaby that put me to sleep each night and woke me early every morning.

In time I would be able to tell exactly what the surf conditions were like, the size and shape, tide and wind conditions, just by listening to the sounds it made.

The surf would come to take my heart and soul, as well as become my life story.

It got into my very bones and has become as much a part of me as my blood. It pulses through my veins. When it's up I can feel the excitement rush through me like a freight train. When it's down I get restless.

Our house was B-21. Next door, in B-20, there was an older guy who was a surfer and whose name was Larry Conroy. He had a beautiful wooden surfboard that he kept in his backyard. I could see it through the slits in the wood fence that bordered our yards. I had wanted to try and ride it for the first few months we lived there.

My dad had bought me a heavy-duty canvas air mattress to ride in the surf. I loved that thing, even though it would rub my body raw daily with its rough and abrasive surface. There were a few other kids along the beach that were my age and we all rode those air matts together. Actually, we would ride anything we could find that would float.

Old pieces of plywood with nails sticking out of them, inner-tubes, whatever. One dude paddled out in a rotten old rowboat we found on the beach one day.

Before he got very far from the beach the thing just sank out from below him, which was really entertaining for the rest of us. The beach and ocean were our playground.

I could not stay out of the water, it drew me like a goddess with a magic flute. The older guys had surfboards. In those days they were made of wood, mostly balsa wood but some still with redwood and other wood combinations. Needless to say, they were heavy. Most of the guys just left them laying around on the beach after they surfed. Nobody was gonna bother them.

Larry Conroy was the best surfer on our beach and he had the nicest surfboard, I guess that's why he kept it in his yard. Right where I could see it and crave riding it. I would peer through that fence day in and day out just wondering what it would be like to be standing on top of it riding some monster wave. It sort of became an obsession after a while, like I was stalking it or something.

Larry had a younger cousin named Kerry, who was my age. Kerry was really good at getting me into trouble. One day we were hanging out, and I was telling him how I wished I could try out that surfboard that Larry had.

He kind of casually, and challenging at the same time, suggested that I might as well just get it over with and sneak the board out of the yard and try it out.

"Larry's not home, nobody will ever know," he urged. "Come on Corky, just do it." Did he later work for Nike?

So, I did.

That was the day my future college career went out the window.

Surfside had a little street that ran along the beach. The houses on the ocean side were "A row." On the land side they were "B row." Our house was on the inland side of the street but there were no houses directly across the street on the beach side. There was also very little beach, maybe only about twenty feet of sand and then the ocean. Kerry had to help me carry the board out of the yard, across the street and onto the beach. It was too heavy for me to pick up by myself.

We were only like six years old at the time and this big wooden surfboard weighed more than both of us together. But we got it down to the water and I made my launch. The surf was probably about three or four feet that day. Although in my boy-mind memory it was freaking huge. Like eighty or ninety feet, maybe a hundred. Really big.

I am really not sure how I made it out past the waves. Must have just been sheer luck. But there I was, sitting on Larry Conroy's beautiful balsa-wood surfboard outside the surf and living life large. What a beautiful feeling and beautiful view. When the waves would pick me up I could see over the houses.

There was a seafood restaurant on the other side of Pacific Coast Highway, which was right behind our house, named "Sam's." Sam's had a big neon fish sign on its roof and I could see it from the board when I would float over wave crests. This was breathtaking.

But the idea was to ride this thing, not just sit there basking in the flora and fauna and enjoying the view.

What I had not counted on was the current. I had floated a little bit north up the beach and without really realizing it I was now out in front of a couple of houses that were on A row. The front of the houses on A row were on wooden pilings keeping them out of the water. That's how short the beach was.

A large wave came along and I decided it was time to try this out. Taking off on an air matt was one thing, you were laying down and they were floaty and full of air. On a surfboard there was way more speed and they are long and pointed. As this mountain of water lifted me skyward, I paddled my guts out and caught it. I leaped to my feet just like I had seen the older guys do a zillion times and prepared to take the drop.

What a rush.

But, as often happens on people's first attempt at this, the nose of the board buried into the bottom of the wave and sprung me off like a large springboard.

Booiiing!!!

I remember looking straight at a house right in front of me as I was flying through the air. Uh oh.

Lucky for me I came out of the bone-crushing wipe out unscathed. But Larry's board didn't fare so well. It had hit one of the pilings under the house and had a giant gash in one rail.

I was in deep cat poo poo. Cat poo poo is much like doggie doo doo but smells worse.

Conferring with Kerry we came up with the only workable solution that seemed available at the time. We would put the board back and never say a word.

This started a sort of bad pattern of behavior for me. I became obsessed with learning to ride surfboards. When the older dudes would leave their boards lying around on the beach and go home, I would sneak them out into the surf and often times would not return them in as good of condition as when I took them.

Rumors ran rampant and eventually I was busted as the bad boy board bandit of Surfside Colony.

One day all the older dudes got together and went to my dad. They told him that either I get my own surfboard or they were going to drown me.

I am not sure how much consideration he gave this choice, but I am sure there was at least one or two chin rubbing "hmmmmms" involved.

On Christmas morning of 1957 I woke up to find my brand new 8'7" balsa wood surfboard laying on our living room floor under the Christmas tree. It weighed 3 pounds more than I did. Perfect.

Christmas time in Southern California is a lot nicer than many places in the world. But even so, it's cold. And that Christmas day was clear and very cold.

None the less I had to try out my new board. It had been hand made by a guy named Dick Barrymore who was a Los Angeles City Fireman that lived in nearby Seal Beach. He made surfboards out of his garage and also surfing and skiing films as a hobby. He would later become very well-known as a leading ski movie maker.

My dad had asked him to make me the board. It was sort of like what a speed shape board would look like today, a little narrow with a "pintail." That means the tail was drawn to a point at the back and is generally used on big wave boards. Why he made me this type of shape I don't know. But I loved it. No, I ADORED it.

The first challenge for me that morning was getting the board across the street and into the water. We had moved up the street to B44, a slightly bigger house with 3 little bedrooms. Mine had a balcony where I could hang out and watch the surf all the time. But it was still on the inland side of the street, so I had to learn how to get my board to the water without dragging it. It was too heavy for me to carry by myself.

I developed the end around end method. I would pick up the tail and move it around to the front, and then the nose and more it around to the front, and eventually I would walk the board down to the water and get on it to paddle out. It wasn't pretty, but it got me there and back.

The actual distance from our yard to the water was probably only about 50 feet at the most, but it was still a job to walk the big wooden surfboard over and back.

On that Christmas morning, I was not to be denied.

I got my new board into the water and launched it on its maiden surf voyage.

Wearing only a pair of swimming trunks, as we had no wetsuits back then, I shivered my way out through the waves and got ready for my first ride. Lucky for me it was very small that morning and there was nobody else around.

I spotted a clean little wave coming my way and went for it. I felt the speed of the board increase as I caught the wave and I jumped to my feet. Wow, there it was. I was standing on my board and racing down the face of the wave towards the left.

My right foot was forward, making me what is called a "goofy-foot," so I was facing the wave. To my amazement I didn't fall when the wave broke. I just kept going all the way to the beach and stepped off.

OH HELL YES!!!!!!!!! I was definitely gonna like this.

For a surfer, your first surfboard is much like your first car or your first lover.

You remember every curve, every line, every detail.

You remember the feel as she moved through the water, the agony of getting her first scratch and the smell of resin the first time you patched her.

I loved my first board and took great care of her. From the point on her nose to the wood burned "Barrymore" hand-done label on the tail. She had a pine skeg (surfboard fin). I rode her hard and definitely put her away wet.

As time went on surfboards were all starting to be made out of polyurethane foam and soon balsa wood would become a material of the past. I am just glad I was one of the lucky ones who learned on a wood board.

CHAPTER TWO

"The Stoke"

From that first Christmas morning until I was out of the house and on my own, my parents had a very hard time keeping me out of the surf. Probably something like ninety percent of my thoughts were centered around surfing. The other ten percent was divided into the various activities of a young boy. Eating, school, friends and what was on television. I don't think my schoolwork suffered much because of my surfing, but probably my social life did to some extent.

From day one, surfing took priority over just about everything else. I was lucky to live right on the beach where I could surf almost as much as I pleased. I could get up before first light and get in a good hour of surfing before catching the school bus.

One of the real struggles I had with my mom was that she had been in music when she was younger and wanted me to learn to play the piano. This was probably because we had a piano, it had come with the house.

She had been a singer during the days of live radio and had performed on KHJ, in Los Angeles, and also had made a couple of records. They were made of tin back then.

Every now and then we would try and play one on our record player, and even though the sound was very scratchy you could hear her and recognize her voice. She had been much younger then, as she had me at close to forty years old.

I have an older sister, Norma, who is twenty years older than I am and was already married with kids of her own when I was born.

None the less mom was always singing when I was a kid and I knew the songs on her records by heart. Her brother, my uncle Lawrence, was a classical violinist and also a jazz drummer who had the band that played on the "Great White Steamship" that traveled back and forth from Long Beach harbor to Catalina Island back in the 1940s.

So, mom wanted me to have music too, and she hired Mrs. Suplee, the wife of a local minister, to give me piano lessons. I might have gotten into it if Mrs. Suplee would have given me anything that I was interested in, in the way of music, to learn. But she was into classical music and insisted that is what I had to learn. I was thinking Ray Charles and she was thinking Bach.

Plus, these piano lessons took place right after I got home from school when my mind was completely focused on getting back into the surf. I resisted to the max, but mom won out, and I was forced to have to bang my way through thirty minutes of practice every day before I could go surfing plus my lesson every Tuesday.

Little did I know then what a solid my Mom was doing for me. One that would come in handy in my post-surf years, and to this day, still does.

Then there was the homework issue. I was pretty good at snowing her into believing that I got all that done right after dinner and before television.

Most of the time I was really hard at work, drawing surf pictures or coming up with cool color schemes for fantasy surfboards that I had in my head. Some homework must have gotten done because I kept my grades reasonable, but I don't remember putting much effort into that.

*　*　*

Something that had a profound effect on me was seeing my first surfing movie. There were a couple of brothers who lived down the street from us named Mike and Marc De Cheveroux.

They were fellow air matt warriors with me and also were getting into surfing at the same time as I was.

Their mom, Ruth, was a huge fan of the bullfights and would head down to Mexico all the time for that. She would also occasionally pile us all in the back of her station wagon and take us surfing down the coast to Doheny and San Onofre, excellent surf spots at the southern end of Orange County.

One night she found out about a "surfing film" being shown at a little artsy kinda theater up in Hollywood and loaded us all up to go see it.

The name of the movie was "Surf Safari."

It was filmed and narrated by a dude named John Severson, who would later go on to publish "SURFER Magazine."

I will never forget the adrenaline rush I felt when the big wave sequence came on the screen. The music got cranked up. It was the Theme from Peter Gunn by Henry Mancini. And the narration went, "On December 15th the biggest swell to hit the Hawaiian Islands in over 50 years came marching out of the North Pacific.

"Only a handful of the, truly hardcore were there to meet the challenge." My jaw dropped, and I was totally swept away with the enormity of this. I was "STOKED" to the max.

I had a full-blown case of surf fever! (a later John Severson movie title).

That did it. From then on I went to see every surf film there was and collected every surf photo, surf poster, surf anything I could get my little hands on.

All the walls in my room and the ceiling would eventually be filled with surf stuff.

Surfing consumed my life.

Yeah, I still played little league baseball and all that kinda stuff, but it was surfing that became my passion. Everything else took back seat to that.

In 1959 the movie "Gidget" hit theaters all around the country. It was based on a real chick who had hung out at Malibu during the summers and had become part of the surf pack there. Her father had written a book about her and the surf crew and it became a Hollywood movie.

Like everything else that had anything to do with surfing, I couldn't wait to go see it. A lot of the local surfers thought it was not very realistic, but I loved it.

Some of the big-name surf stars did the surfing in it, like Mickey Dora. A dude named Mickey Munoz, who is a little guy himself, did some of the surfing for Sandra Dee (Gidget) wearing a girls' two- piece bathing suit and a blonde wig.

The rest was done by Linda Benson, the top female surfer in the world, in those days.

That movie had a HUGE impact on surfing.

Before that, the entire surfing population in the United States consisted of a few pockets of what were considered "beatniks," "bohemians" and "lunatics" along the west coast and in Hawaii.

After the "Gidget" movie, all surf-hell broke loose. Everybody wanted to be a surfer!

America had this romantic notion that surfers were all free-spirited party-loving nomads that didn't work and spent all their time surfing and making out with hot chicks at beach parties and in the backs of their "Woodys."

This was an image that I could definitely sink my teeth into and grasp it as a workable vision to ascend to. I was as stoked as a kid could be.

CHAPTER THREE

"I'm Gonna be Good... and... I Don't Care What You Think"

With the gaining popularity of surfing, came surfing publications.

One day, somebody at school told me that there was a surfing newspaper that had come out and had a killer photo of three guys on a giant wave at Makaha, Hawaii, on the cover.

The word was that they had them for sale at the Ole Surfboard shop in Sunset Beach, about a half-mile south of our house.

When I got home I squealed, whined and begged my mom relentlessly until she coughed up a dollar.

Then, I jumped on my trusty Schwinn three-speed and flew down the road as fast as my little legs could peddle.

The Ole Surfboards shop was an old Quonset hut converted into a tiny showroom in front, with the entire manufacturing process done in the back.

That was back in the days of real surf shops.

You got blasted by the smell of resin right when you went through the door. And, normally you would step in some and ruin your shoes at the same time, or at least get a bad case of fiberglass itch from the dust in the air from sanding the boards. It was sort of becoming a part of the whole process I guess. Be one with your board, so to speak.

When I got to the shop that day local surf star, and future legendary lifeguard, Timmy Dorsey was working in the little sales area. He was one of my surfing heroes at that time and I was happy that he was there to talk to. Little did I know then that Tim would become a lifelong friend and brother, to this day.

Timmy was one of the few local surf stars who had taken the time to be nice to me in the water and always had a smile and a "hey kid, howzit?" for me.

Of course, I was probably a bit hard to bear at that time for most of them due to my zealous stoke and high energy. More on that a bit later.

So, Timmy sees me come in and gets this huge grin on his face. "I bet I know what yoooooouuuuu want," he said with music in his voice.

My eyes lit up. There it was sitting on the counter. The object of my desires.

The first surfing newspaper complete with the classic surf shot of Peter Cole, Wally Forsyth and George Downing screaming across this huge and beautiful wall of water at Makaha.

"Yeah, the paper, the paper, the PAAAAPPPPPEEEEEEEEER. I WANT IT." I bellowed with glee.

"How much money do ya got?"

"My mom gave me a dollar, is that enough?"

At first Tim sort of winched and frowned. He was looking at the ground and kinda shaking his head.

I guess he could see the light go out in my eyes. Well, I guess he kind of engineered that actually. "Gee kid, they want a buck and a half for this thing," he said with just a touch of sympathy in his tone.

My head dropped.

"But for you, I will let this one here with only the small resin drip on the corner and a light mustard stain from my sandwich, go for only a dollar."

"REEEEEALLLLY????" I came back to life.

"Yep. And not only that, I also want to tell you that Ole and I have been watching you surf and are impressed with what we have been seeing. You could have some potential."

"REEEEEALLLLLY?????" My heart was soaring. (Note: The price on the cover was actually fifty cents.)

"Yep. And Ole has authorized me to offer you a surf team deal if you wanna ride an Ole Surfboard."

"REEEEEEALLLLLLLY??????"

"Yep. Free color."

"FREEEEE COLOR... OH WOW... REEEEEALLY???"

"Yep. So, when do ya wanna order your new team Ole board amigo?"

Before those words had finished leaving Timmy's lips I was on my bike, slightly soiled surfing newspaper in hand, and was racing home as fast as I could go. My dad should be getting home from work at any minute and I had some serious work to do.

At that time I had just about completely thrashed my second board.

It had started out to be a candy apple red tint foam board made by the same Dick Barrymore who had made my first balsa wood board.

The wood board had lasted me about a year and a half and then I had to have one of the new "foam" boards. It was the thing. Lighter and more maneuverable.

I was about a year and a half into the candy apple red Barrymore, which was now a weird faded yellow-brown kinda color, and it was so full of dings and patches that the original lightweight red beauty had turned into a heavy sluggish eyesore.

Even my dad could see that.

I have to say that both of my parents were always behind my surfing and did all they could to support me. When I told my dad about the "surf team deal" his eyebrows went up.

"Free color, that's a good deal?" he smiled.

"Yeah Dad, amazing deal! Ole and Timmy Dorsey himself think I have potential. Come on dad, pleeeeeeaaassssssssee????????"

This conversation when on for about a month until he finally caved in and agreed to buy me the board. But I had to pay him back half of what it cost from my paper route. I think the "free color" price was $80. So I owed him forty bucks.

This was sort of the beginning of him trying to teach me the value of things.

The day I ordered my first Ole still stands out in my dimly lit memory banks.

Tim and I went over a few different color combinations and it was an agonizing process.

A friend of mine who started surfing about the same time as I did, named Terry O'Dell, had a board with a topless mermaid painted on the nose, which I thought was extremely cool.

But, my mom might not like that.

After a while I finally settled on three color panels. Green, White, and Red. Tim pointed out that this would look like a big Mexican flag.

"Well, then I can yell "Ol'e" (like the bullfight call) on my Oleeeee," I announced.

This was like a strange omen for things to come later in both of our lives which I will get to when I get to that part of this story.

One of my fondest memories of that first Ole board was one day when I was surfing in front of our house and there was a high tide running.

As I mentioned earlier, the houses on the ocean side of the street were on pilings and at high tide the surf actually went under the houses. Kinda like the houses were on little piers or something. Across the street from our house was a single-story home owned by Mr. and Mrs. Kray.

Just to the south of their house, was a break of about six lots until the next house that was on pilings which was owned by the Hendershots.

On this particular day, I was riding a wave and came into the shorebreak right between the two houses. Just as the wave closed out near the sand I did what was called a "fly away kickout." That is where you launch your board towards the sky to get yourself out of the wave.

When I came up I looked all around me and could not find my board.

My dad was standing on the street watching me at the time. He was a short and stocky kinda dude with curly hair and blue eyes. He loved to fish but he never learned to swim.

He was standing there with a kinda pissed off look on his face. "Hey dad, did you see where my board went?" I called out.

He pointed toward the Krays house. Uh oh. There was my board sticking out of the Krays kitchen window.

I had launched it so high that it cleared their porch railing and went right through the glass window and into their kitchen sink. Only the tail end was sticking out.

"Oops!"

* * *

Being a team rider, of sorts, definitely bolstered my fresh young and growing surf ego. And made me even more convinced than I had been before that I was going to surf and surf and surf, and one day become a surf star like Timmy Dorsey and the guys who I had seen in the surf movies, and in that mustard stained surfing newspaper.

My little mind had begun to focus itself like it had no other purpose. When I saw somebody who surfed better than I did I would watch them and try to copy some aspect of their surfing that I liked. A turn or cutback or the way they held their arms.

***

One day I'll never forget, was when I saw Robert August surf in front of my house. He was wearing white trunks and had a light blue board. I thought that was totally cool looking and was thinking about painting my board light blue.

About then, I saw one of Bud Browne's surf movies and had flipped out over the surfing of Phil Edwards and Dewey Weber. Phil was ultra-casual and Dewey was ultra-radical.

I wanted to surf like Phil but look like Dewey.

He had worn white trunks and had a red board in the movie. So then I wanted to paint my board red.

The farthest I got was to take an old pair of my dads' white "clam- diggers" and cut them off just above the knees. They had a couple of blue strips down the sides of the legs which I thought was cool. This made a sort of a baggy looking kind of surf trunks. Once clad in my white "baggies" I set out to try and surf like a sort of makeshift Phil Edwards/Dewey Weber combo. Two opposites.

I think what I got was an over exaggerated arm waving nonstop motor mouthed surfing energizer bunny.

When the hot local guys would show up to surf in front of my house, which was really the best spot in our local area, I would be all over them like a sand flea on a beach dog.

"Hey you guys, gonna go out????

Huh Huh... Wow, it's looking really good. (It was horrible). Hey, I'll meetcha out there.

I wanna show you my new monster Dewey Weber drop knee cutback and really cool Phil Edwards head bobble.

"Wow." I would babble.

Usually by the time I changed and grabbed my board from the backyard they had driven away in haste. But sometimes they would go out and I probably bugged the heck out of them.

I wanted to be good and I really didn't care who knew it or what they thought about it.

Then came the day that the first issue of SURFER Magazine came out.

I was at school when I found out about it. A pal of mine named Greg Hector had one.

Everybody was trying to get a look at it during lunch.

Greg told me that Robert August had ten of them for sale and I had better get over to Robert's house right after school if I wanted to get one.

Same deal as with the newspaper.

I got home and begged and pleaded with my mom to give me the $1.50 that the magazine cost. But she only had a five-dollar bill and told me that I had to bring home the change. No problemo mama. I jumped on the trusty three-speed Schwinn and raced the mile or so over to Robert August's mint green house on 13th Street and Seal Way in Seal Beach. I did NOT wanna miss out on getting my copy.

When I knocked on the door Robert's dad, the legendary Blackie August, answered the door.

Blackie was one of the real surf dudes from the early days of wooden boards.

"Wow, Blackie August... wowie wowie," I stammered.

Blackie just smiled and looked at me. "Uh, is Robert home?" I managed to spit out.

"Yeah, he's down the hall in his room jacking off," Blackie said with a wave towards a slightly ajar door down the hallway.

Jacking off? Was he serious or just joking? Geeze, did I dare go down there? Yes, I wanted my SURFER Magazine. Besides, Blackie had to be kidding, right?"

WRONG. I sheepishly knocked on Roberts door and kinda peeked in at the same time. Ahhhhh man..... there was Robert.... jacking off.

I was living the Southwest Airlines commercial "Want to Get Away?"

"Whadda ya want Carroll?" Robert bellowed while pulling up his, yes white, surf trunks.

"I wanna buy a *SURFER Magazine*, that's all." "Ya got any money?"

"Yeah, my mom gave me five dollars but I have to take home the change."

"Change? There is no change you punk. They cost five dollars." "But it says $1.50 on the cover Robert?"

"Well, that's before shipping and handling charges and my commission. If ya want one, it's five dollars. Take it or leave it."

Naturally I took it.

I did get my mother's money's worth though. I have to admit that I read that magazine over and over and looked at those photos until my eyes must have faded them half off the pages. I had every photo in my mind, every caption, every word in every ad, on every page.

Thinking back, that magazine must have originally been a promotion for John Severson's next surfing movie, *"Surf Fever,"* because all the photos were from the film.

Maybe he had intended it to be a program, but it had grown into a magazine, so he decided to release it as one. In any case, it was a good move. Before long, *SURFER Magazine* would become the official bible of surfing.

CHAPTER FOUR

"Competition and Pre-Pro Years"

The first big surfing competition in California in what is called the "Modern Era" of surfing, (starting the late 1950's with the advent of the polyurethane foam surfboards).

It was the "West Coast Surfing Championships" held at the Huntington Beach Pier in September of 1959. I was eleven years old.

I got my dad to take me down there so I could surf the Junior Men's division, which was seventeen and under.

The surf was pretty big that weekend and I was pretty scared.

There were six surfers in my heat and they were all 16 or 17 and they all were confident and cool looking. I managed to take third in the heat. Not good enough to advance but good enough to give me a little boost of encouragement.

The highlight of the weekend for me was sitting on the pier all day Sunday and watching all the big-name surf stars competing right there in front of my very eyes.

The big winner was Jack Haley, one of our local surf heroes from Seal Beach.

After it was over we saw Jack in the parking lot getting into his car and I went over to say congratulations.

He was very humble about it and surprised me by saying he had seen my heat and that I looked pretty good, to stick with it and one day I would win a trophy.

WIN A TROPHY?????

Wow, what a concept that was.

This was right before the offer for the "team deal free color" from Timmy Dorsey and Ole.

After that event, many smaller surfing competitions started happening all up and down the west coast.

By hook, crook, or even hitch-hiking, I managed to enter and surf in every one of them. I never got past the first round though.

None the less I was not deterred.

One day I was gonna take home a trophy, Jack Haley had told me so and I fully bought into it.

I was probably the only person who knew this beyond any shadow of a doubt.

I surfed morning, noon and night. It didn't matter what the conditions were, I surfed it. I'm sure I rode more junky terrible waves than anybody else had up to that point.

The surf in front of my house was good in the mornings and horrible and windy in the afternoons. Sometimes it had good form but most of the time it didn't. I got to where I could tell what the surf was like without even opening my eyes in the morning.

I could tell by the sound and the feel of the vibrations on my bed and wall next to my bed. To actually see it I had to open my eyes and lift my head a few inches to look out the window.

The one sound I dreaded and never wanted to hear was the foghorn.

That horrid low drone "uuouu – uuouu."

It meant that it was foggy. Fog was like the worst condition. No matter how the surf was it didn't matter because you could not see anything.

You could ride bad waves, deal with wind and rain, big or small. But fog was a real dilemma.

I could not hear the sound of fog.

Living next to the navy base at Seal Beach had the extra added advantage that they had a very powerful foghorn to warn the ships that they were near the jetties that bordered the harbor.

* * *

My second "team deal" came about a year and a half later when a guy named Larry Weiss, aka "The Crow," opened a small shop in the back of the boat cover building that was across Pacific Coast Highway, behind my house.

Crow was one of those dudes that looked exactly like his nickname. He had black hair and a big hairy black beard and mustache. The rumor was that he was a great surfboard shaper.

He had a guy working for him named Roy Crump. Roy had become one of the more or less "locals" who hung out and surfed near my house.

Down the street, there was a big old wooden water tower. It was right at the end of our private beach colony and sort of was the border between Surfside and Sunset Beach.

It was legal to park on the road in Sunset Beach, so "Water Tower" was pretty much the local surf spot.

The surf was usually better the block up in front of my house, but most of the surf traffic was in front of the water tower. Roy was part of a group of guys who would come down from Long Beach to surf at the water tower a lot of the time.

Usually, I would surf in front of my house early in the morning before anybody got there and then after breakfast walk down to "water tower" to surf and hang out with that crew. I was in need of other surfers to talk to in those days.

I do vividly remember one morning down at the Water Tower when things did not go so well for me in that department.

Robert August had shown up along with Bill Fury. Robert was the hot kid in the Seal Beach area and so was Fury.

They were about 4 years older than me and already had reputations for their surfing skills.

Fury and just come out of the water with his brand-new Dewey Weber board and I asked him if I could try it. He was always really cool and said sure, so I paddled it out and caught a few waves on it. I was riding an 8'2" at the time, and Bills board was maybe 9'6."

When I came in I commented that it felt like a great board, but I wasn't used to one so long.

Robert August, as sarcastic as they come, loudly says, to me and the whole beach, "Naw Carroll, you are just too shitty to ride it."

What had just happened? Robert August, THE Robert August, had just rudely insulted my surfing in front of everybody. I didn't know what to say, I was in shock.

So, I took my board and sadly walked home alone.

My mom saw the look on my face and asked me what had happened, there might have been a tear or two involved.

I just told her I had a bad day surfing and left it at that, for the moment.

This little bit of cruelty stuck with me and I vowed to one day get my revenge on freaking Robert August. (Or maybe it was my payback for interrupting him in the heat of the moment.)

* * *

One day I walked over to check out this new Crow Surfboards shop and Roy was there. He introduced me to the Crow.

Crow told me that he wanted me to help him get all the locals riding his boards and offered me pretty much the same deal as Timmy Dorsey had for Ole.

However, in this case I could also have any sort of "stringer" arrangement I wanted as well as color.

Stringers are the wood strips that go down the surfboard for strength. It cost a lot more to have a board with more than one stringer and it looked very cool.

So once again I was off to make the deal with my dad so I could order my new Crow surfboard.

I went way overboard on that one. I ordered it with ten stringers and all sorts of pastel colors.

In those days the color was mostly done with pigments in the final gloss coat and it made the board heavier. Ten stringers had already made it very heavy and when all the color was added what I wound up with was a very wild looking board that weighed as much as a small barge.

It did do one good thing for my surfing though. It smoothed me out a little bit. It was hard to turn with all that weight.

* * *

One day when I was over there seeing if my new board was done yet, did I mention it took about four months for it to be finished, I decided to stop into the boat cover shop.

The guy who owned it was a dude named Walter Katin.

Walter wore a captain's hat, had a beard and sort of looked like a "Jolly Roger" kinda seaman. You expected a parrot on his shoulder or something.

At that time there was no surfwear industry. There was basically no "surfwear."

T-shirts with surfboard maker logos was about it. Maybe surf club jackets or sweatshirts. There were a couple of "custom surf trunks" business's in Hawaii.

One was M. Nee out at Makaha and the other was Take in Waikiki. In California there wasn't much.

John Wilkes mom made a few for him and his pals in Laguna Beach.

So, I decided to ask Walter Katin if he could make me a custom pair of surf trunks.

Walt said he could make anything and asked me to do a drawing of what surf trucks should look like. The best I had was sort of a version of the cut off clam diggers that I had been wearing. Longer than "swim trunks" and with a lace up front. This was before Velcro.

Walter's wife, Nancy, measured me and about a week later I had my first pair of Kanvas by Katin custom surf trunks. It was their first pair too. They fit me perfectly and looked great. Red canvas. The only problem was that boat canvas is very heavy and stiff.

They weighed a ton when wet and were so stiff that they could stand up by themselves when you weren't wearing them. They also gave me a horrible rash.

So, I went back to Walter and told him that these were great but that the canvas was too heavy and stiff.

He said they had a softer cotton material that I think Nancy was going to make some curtains for their boat out of. It was called "sharkskin." And it was white.

So, they made me another pair out of that and they were fantastic.

Everybody wanted to know where I got them. I sent them all over to the boat cover shop to order their own custom-made surf trunks.

Soon Walter and Nancy were making way more surf trunks than boat covers and put up a Kanvas by Katin Custom Surf Trunks sign over the front door.

They eventually became the largest "custom" surf trunks company in the world. I could always get a free pair.

* * *

One day we had a huge swell and some dude lost his board into the rocks near the jetty at the north end of the beach. It was a balsawood Hobie and it was getting thrashed. The dude was afraid to go down into the rocks to get it. I asked him what he was going to do with it and he said it was worthless now and wasn't worth risking his life to retrieve. I asked him if I could have it if I went and got it.

He said he didn't care and if I wanted to die in the crab covered rocks with monster shorebreak pounders crashing into them it was cool with him.

That was the last I ever saw of that dude. I have no idea who he was.

I hung out for a while and waited for the tide to go down. When it did, and the waves stopped pounding into the rocks, I went down and got what was left of the board.

Here in my hot little kid hands was the chance to actually build my own board. I could strip off the old fiberglass, let the wood dry out and then reshape it into a new board.

A (cue in angels singing and halleluiahs) "Corky Board." I was giddy with glee and had visions of this perfect and beautiful work of art and craftsmanship that would shock and impress all my friends and burst me onto the scene as a surfboard builder.

Never mind that I was not old enough for a woodshop class at school yet nor did I have any idea whatsoever on how to shape and fiberglass a surfboard. I would figure it out.

So, I scrounged around for a couple of old sawhorses and got a small hand plainer out of my dad's toolbox and went to work on my creation.

The shape did not come out all that bad either. It was 7'10" long and in retrospect resembled what a speed shape would have looked like, say for small surf in Hawaii, around the early 1970s.

The fiber glassing was a whole nother story. I only knew how to use fiberglass to patch small dings in my boards. To actually glass a whole board was beyond me. So, I did it in parts.

I glassed a third of the bottom, then another and then the other. Then did the same thing with the top. NOT having a power sander did not help either. I tried to hand sand the thing, which was rampant with sharp edges but didn't do even close to a good job. Finally, I put about six gloss coats over the top in order to cover up all the edges and bumps. I had fiberglass itch for years after making that board.

But the all-time best mistake I made was putting on the fin. I didn't know how to keep it standing up straight while I was attaching it to the board with resin.

The best plan I could come up with was to put two bricks on each side of it to hold it in place while the resin was drying. I did this one night and had visions of taking it out for its maiden voyage the next morning.

But, when I went to get it ready to surf the fin fell off and the bricks were stuck solid to the board instead. This made my pal Steve Rowe, who was with me that morning, very happy. He laughed so hard he cried. I just cried without the laughing.

It was a sad, yet when looking back, extremely funny moment. "How do you think it will surf with bricks instead of a fin?" Eventually I got the bricks off and the fin on and surfed the board.

It worked pretty well even though the glass job was so ugly and bad that it was far from the amazing work of surf art that I had originally envisioned.

The upside was that, one way or another, my days of surfboard and surfwear design had sprouted their early roots.

As I mentioned earlier, I was doing my best to surf in every big or little surfing completion I could find. I would see all the top surfers and watch them intently. I was a student of surfing and surf contests were the classroom. My front yard was study hall.

There was not much else on my mind. Until I met Theresa Thompson.

* * *

Theresa became my first real girlfriend. We met in seventh grade when we sat next to each other in class. But it wasn't until her family moved to Dana Point later in the year that we actually got close.

I used to ride the Greyhound bus down there to visit her on the weekends. It was during those visits that I fell in love with the Dana Point and San Clemente area.

"South County." Dana Point had a beautiful cove which I had surfed a couple of times on "surf safaris" in the back of my dad's pickup truck or with Mrs. DeCheveroux and her sons.

Theresa and I would walk from the cove south to Doheny State Park on little trails through the rocks and tide pools. It was very romantic.

At Doheny the surf was always good in the afternoons due to the fact that the winds would come across Dana Point and blow offshore at Doheny. All the hot surfers in the area would be there every afternoon.

Theresa's best friend was Marianne Harrison, the daughter of legendary waterman Lorin Harrison. One day when we were down there Marianne introduced me to mega surfing star Mickey Munoz.

Mickey was very nice and seemed to have this constant smile and laugh going on. I liked him right off the bat. Years later we talked about that meeting and he never remembers it. But I did.

It was also on one of my surf/romance trips to visit Theresa and surf Doheny that I met Mike Doyle. Mike was already a superstar in all the movies and magazines.

I was hitchhiking home, due to the fact that I had spent my bus money on buying lunch for Theresa and was standing on Pacific Coast Highway in front of the entrance to Doheny when Mike came driving by and picked me up.

I could NOT even believe I was getting a ride from one of the most famous surfers in the world. I jumped into the passenger seat and bellowed out, "OH MY GOD, MIKE DOYLE!" He got this look on his face that said, "uh oh, maybe this wasn't such a good idea." For the next hour I talked his ear off.

Years later talking about this first meeting he DID remember it. He said it was the reason he quit picking up hitchhiking surfers unless they were chicks.

* * *

1962 was an extreme "year of change" for me. I got my first total surfboard sponsorship from Richard Harbour, of Harbour Surfboards in Seal Beach, early that year. Rich was just getting going making boards but his shapes had already become popular with the locals in the area. He was the first to offer me free boards to surf for him.

Rich was a tall dude who surfed himself and was a fellow "goofy- foot" (stands right foot forward) like myself. Besides making me a very fine surfboard, Rich took me surfing at Cotton's Point for the first time. It was the beginning of a long-time love affair between myself and that surf spot.

From the first wave I rode there I had this feeling that God had designed that surf spot with me in mind. It was thick and powerful and was a fairly perfectly shaped left. Not a point break as much as what you would call a reef break. The bottom is made up of round river rocks that came from the San Mateo Creek just to the south.

That area is known for its series of amazing surfing spots starting with Cotton's Point at the north and including Upper and Lower Trestles, Church and San Onofre Surf Beach at the south. There is something very special about that stretch of beaches, a wave quality not found in many areas and certainly one of the very best on the California coast.

Corky Carroll – Not Done Yet

Rich made me a very beautiful purple and white 8'6" that I absolutely loved. I had a pair of white surf trunks that the Katins had made for me that had four dark blue strips going down the sides of the legs.

The combo of the board and trunks gave me a very cool kinda "look." It was sort of like the first time you have a set of clothes that you really feel like you look good in, even if you don't.

It makes you feel cool. Well that board and trunks combo made me feel cool and maybe it also made me surf better because I was feeling cool.

Whatever the case, in the summer of 1962 I won my first surfing contest on that board and in those trunks.

It was the San Clemente Surf Capades and I won the Jr. Men's (under 18) division. I was 14. Not only was it my first contest win, it was also the first time I had ever even won my preliminary heat, much less the whole contest.

To say I was happy about this would not even come close to describing the way I was feeling when they announced my name as the winner.

I was in surf gremmie heaven. All these big-name surf dudes came up and congratulated me, including Mike Doyle and Mickey Munoz, and said I surfed really well. What an amazing day.

Rich Harbour had driven me to the contest along with another hot young surfer from Seal Beach named Danny Lenahan. Danny was also riding a Harbour board and had taken third place. We were happy kids on that ride home.

I remember that I had Rich let me off down at the end of our street, by the big water tower, so I could show all of our neighbors my trophy on the way home. I was one proud puppy.

Winning that first contest pretty much changed my life. All of a sudden I was at least semi-known.

I started winning most all of the small contests up and down the coast in the junior men's division and some of the "club" contests where there were no divisions. I now had the confidence that I could win and that made the real difference.

Corky Harbour Surfboards ad. Photo: Robert "Smitty" Von Sternberg.

When you actually do something for the first time, and realize that you CAN do that, it makes you think about it differently. Also, it was the first time my picture was in *SURFER Magazine*. It was in an ad for Harbour that featured myself and Richard Chew, the groundwork for my surfing career was now being laid.

Corky Carroll – Not Done Yet

* * *

In early 1963 Hobie bought out OLE Surfboards and opened an OLE shop on Bay Boulevard in Seal Beach. It was in the downstairs part of my pal Scott Hoxeng's house.

Hobie was the biggest and most respected surfboard builder in the world. He hired Mickey Munoz to manage the shop and run OLE Surfboards.

The first thing Mickey did was recruit me to surf on an OLE. That was one of those bittersweet agonizing moments in my surf career that I always remembered.

I really liked Richard Harbour and he had been very good to me while I rode his boards. But he was small and local and Hobie was the big time.

Mickey talked to my parents and convinced them, and me, that being under the Hobie umbrella would mean huge benefits to my surfing career.

It's kinda funny looking back at that now.

There was no such thing as a professional surfer then, but none the less I was positive that I was gonna be one.

And going with Hobie seemed like the best decision for that very reason. But it was sad for me too. I kinda felt like it was like breaking up with the nice homely girl in favor of the hot flashy one. Of course, it proved to be the right thing in the long run, and my "career" was put into a higher gear right off the bat.

Rich went on to become a master shaper and surfboard builder who is respected the world over for his quality work, still making boards to this day.

But at that moment, at that crossroads, I had to go with Hobie even though it was a really gut-wrenching thing to do.

Mickey became my mentor and took me to all the surfing events.

He got me into paddleboard races that I had never considered before. I was good at it and won all the races. This, in fact, helped my surfing and my competitive success.

The guy who catches the best waves usually wins, that fact is still in effect today for the most part.

Mickey took me to Malibu and introduced me to all sorts of great people in the surfing world. He also took care of me and was real big on right and wrong and telling me to shut up when I needed it.

My favorite part of hanging out with him was his great laugh and sense of humor. I love that. I would have loved to have been a stand-up comedian if surfing hadn't taken me first. I had a sense of humor too, unfortunately, some people didn't get that and would take some things seriously that I had said in jest. My reaction was typical for a punk surfer. "Hey, if they can't take a joke, fuck 'em!"

Obviously, I had not yet learned the meaning of diplomacy, and, also in fact, maybe I never did get that part right. But I really loved to laugh and a good joke was like breathing fresh air. It makes me feel good to laugh and I always took that road if I had the choice.

Even in anger, I would rather find a way to defuse it by some sort of humor than let it get to me. My beautiful wife Raquel hates that. If she gets mad at me for something and I make a joke she gets even madder.

I have had to learn when and when not to inject humor, and it has taken a lot of years and mistakes along the way to have learned that lesson. IF, I have learned that lesson? (Said with a smirk and laughing, hahahaha).

Corky Carroll – Not Done Yet

At early surfing contest at Hermosa Beach.
Corky 1st place, Mark Martinson 2nd place, Eddie Bonham 3rd place.
Photo: LeRoy Grannis courtesy of John Grannis

* * *

It was on one of the surf trips up to Malibu with Mickey Munoz that I first met the infamous "bad boy of surfing," Mickey Dora.

"The Munoz Mickey" introduced me to, "The Dora Mickey" while we were sitting in the lineup waiting for a wave. He gave me a smile and a "hey kid." That was pretty much it. When I got out of the water I sat on the beach and watched them both surf for quite a while, these were two of the best surfers on the coast and this was their spot. I was soaking it all in like a sponge.

When Dora came out of the water I walked up to him and said something kiss ass like, "Wow man, you were really tearing the place apart."

He looked at me with a big charismatic smile and said, "Thanks kid, hey, can I use your towel a minute."

I had my towel wrapped around my shoulders and immediately said, "sure," and handed it to him.

At that point he blew his nose into it, looked down at it for a moment, then handed it back with a "thanks kid."

He then walked off without another word. I was standing there looking at my snot-filled towel wondering seriously if I should either throw it away or mount it on my wall.

Mickey Munoz also had a huge impact on my surfing and success in competition. He showed me how to go faster on a board. Speed equals momentum and power, which in turn opens up the door for bigger and more fluid maneuvers. My surfing got better and smoother when I learned how to go faster.

Phil Edwards and I started to surf together a little bit about the same time and Mickey suggested that Phil make me a board. He built me this huge 10'7" speed board that weighed a ton and was nearly impossible to turn. He told me if I rode that board for a whole summer it would smooth me out and make me a better surfer.

I remember he said that I spent too much time riding the board and not the wave and that this board would go a long way to helping me learn the difference. Well, if going straight and never turning makes you smoother, it did its job. I became much better at going as fast as possible between point A and point B. Plus, you look a lot smoother when you are standing in one position and never turning.

I was, however, really glad when that lesson was learned and I got to get a smaller board that would actually turn and nose ride.

I did come off that board a better surfer and much more aware of riding the wave ahead of what I was trying to do with the board. Eventually, these two blended themselves together.

Another thing I learned by going to contests with Mickey was strategy.

He was the one who made me get a waterproof watch and time the surf conditions. Waves come in sets. By having an idea of when the best sets would come gives you an advantage to being in the right spot at the right time. And paying attention to the results as they came down to see how the judges were scoring. What was getting the best scores and what each judge seemed to be looking for. I had never looked at it like that. It was always in the mindset to just go out there and surf as good as I could.

Mickey had a much more professional approach to getting the best scores possible. And the best scores win.

Many times that would not represent the guy who surfed the best or looked the best. It was who scored the most points. Think basketball or tennis. Same deal.

It was Mickey Munoz who taught me that.

Right about this same time that I became pals with a kid from Long Beach named Mark Martinson. He was a really good up and coming surfer, only a year older than me and super fun to hang out with.

Mark had also been on hand that day at Water Tower when Robert August had shamed me in front of everybody, I often mentioned to him that one day I was gonna get him back for that.

Mark loved *MAD Magazine* and had the humor to go along with it. His mom used to drop him off at our house to spend weekends a lot of the time. Then when he got his driver's license she would let him take her car to go out in.

This opened up a huge new world of hitting "parties" up and down the coast. South Bay was a major party spot and we used to hit it up there on any given Friday or Saturday night.

My favorite story from these adventures was when we had taken a couple of dates to a party in Redondo Beach and had stopped to "park" someplace on the way home.

Mark's date must have had a bit too much to drink because she barfed all over Mark and the backseat of his mom's car. Not knowing what else to do we got a hose and washed out the back seat, it was pretty gross.

The next day, when Marks mom wanted to know why her back seat was all wet, Mark very calmly, and in sincere and earnest tones told her that we had gone down to check out the surf at "Power Plant," in Seal Beach, and a wave had broken over the car while we were standing on the jetty looking at the waves. He explained that we had accidently left the backdoor open and that's why only the backseat was wet.

The amazing part about this story is that she bought it, hook, line and sinker.

Mark and I would share all kinds of adventures through the years and he remains one of my best friends and favorite people to this day.

CHAPTER 5

"The Turning Point" ~ 1963

By the summer of '63 things had started to change fairly dramatically in my life. Hobie had dissolved Ole Surfboards and I was now firmly on the Hobie Surf Team. This was a lineup of many of the best surfers in the world. I had the one big contest win under my belt and had won a few smaller surf club events up and down the coast.

I talked my parents into letting me spend the summer in Hawaii. I had a friend who I had gone to school with the year before whose father was in the Navy and had been transferred to Pearl Harbor. His name was Mike Ferguson and he had invited me to come stay at his house.

My parents were always good about supporting my surfing addiction and also, for some reason that I could never quite understand, they trusted me way beyond the levels that I should have been trusted.

If they only knew the trouble that I "almost" got into, or "barely missed" getting into.

Somehow, someway, I managed to get away with things that I should not have been able to get away with. Blind luck probably. I am sure everybody has some of this in the history of their youth.

When I got to Mike's house I found that he was about a thirty to forty-minute drive from the place that I wanted to surf. Ala Moana.

The first day I was there I had to wait until the afternoon for Mike to finish summer school before we got to go surfing. In Hawaii, you could drive at 15 and Mike already had his own car. The surf that day was fantastic and I totally fell in love with the short stretch of surf between Kaisers and the Ala Moana bowl on the south shore of Oahu.

In the summer the south swells are good in what they call "town." In the winter the big north and west swells break on the other side of the island, the famed "North Shore." This was summer so I was surfing town mostly, with the occasional trip out to Yokahama Bay, at the far end of the west shore, which picked up south swells and had a ton of power.

It was that day I met two of my all-time surfing idols, even to this day. George Downing and Paul Strauch.

The waves were big, bigger than I was used to anyway. And they had the Hawaiian power and speed which was much more powerful and faster than California waves.

I had taken off on a big set wave and was screaming down the line going as fast as I could go. All of a sudden I was deep in a very dark tunnel and the wave was roaring over my head like a freight train. I panicked and jumped off, in the process, I think I let out a very girlish like scream.

George and Paul had been paddling out and they saw and heard the whole thing. When I came up they were both rolling off their boards laughing.

Geeze, how freaking embarrassing was that. Two of the biggest surf stars on the planet having witnessed THAT. Argh!

To my amazement, when I finished swimming all the way in to get my board, and had paddled back out to the lineup, both of them were super friendly and offered kindish words of encouragement. It was a humbling afternoon to say the least.

That was the beginning of an incredible summer.

A few days went by and I met a dude named Curt Mistalka. Curt lived right across the street from Ala Moana in an apartment building named the Driftwood. He said I could make a bed on his balcony and stay there. He worked at night and slept during the day.

So the deal was I needed to be out of the apartment by about eight in the morning and not come back until late afternoon. Not a problem at all, the surf was right there. So I moved out of Mike's family home and onto the balcony of Curt.

This little fact was never discovered by my parents. Fifteen years old and on the loose in Waikiki for the summer? OH YESSSSSSSSS!!!

My routine was pretty good. I would go for a morning surf and then stash my board in a locker downstairs. Then I would spend about an hour collecting plumeria flowers along the street and making three or four leis. This was easy, all I needed was a sewing needle and some fishing line. Then I would stroll down to the main part of Waikiki and sell the leis to tourists for about five bucks each. Twenty dollars went a long way then.

After that, I would drift into the pool area at the Hilton Hawaiian Village and hang out checking for available young tourist babes.

There were always at least a few basking in the sun on their deck chairs, and who were many times hoping for some young surf dude, such as me, to come along and distract them from their vacation with mom and dad.

Most of the time a few of the right words, and the "look," would result in being asked to lunch. If I played it cool and was nice with the mom and dad, a dinner invitation was pretty much a sure bet.

After that the customary "romantic walk on the beach" many times led its way back to Curt's apartment, which I now had all to myself as he was off to work and wouldn't be back until morning.

The period between lunch and dinner was prime time for surfing. The best surfers were out and the best surfing got done in the later afternoons at Ala Moana.

Normally in the mornings I might surf Kaisers or Rock Pile, but the afternoons were always spent at Ala Moana. God I loved that spot. What a great wave. Fast and hollow and it goes left. For me, being right foot forward (goofy foot), this was paradise.

When I had first got off the plane that summer I was pretty confident that I was becoming a hot surfer.

It took NO time at all surfing Ala Moana to knock me back a whole lotta steps. In that lineup I was definitely NOT so hot. There were guys out there who I had never heard of that were light years ahead of me. Guys that worked all day in the pineapple factory and came out in the late afternoons and just killed it.

It was also a great place to learn how to shut up and stay under the radar. It is very "local" out there.

A loud-mouthed "hoale" gets evicted quickly. I guess being 15 helped out and some of the older dudes cut me some slack. Also surfing for Hobie was a huge plus.

One of the guys who surfed for Hobie over there was Eddie Aikau. He and I hit it off really well and I was invited to the Aikau home for dinner a couple of times.

It was a real honor to be treated with such warm hospitality by this great Hawaiian family. Eddie, as most people know, went on to become one of the greatest big wave surfers in history, and his little brother Clyde was close behind.

My first week on the south shore was when I learned quickly about big-headed surfers coming over from California. When I was getting my board made for that trip I was told to have my name put on it because boards got stolen a lot over there.

So I asked for that, thinking that they would simply write my name on the stringer. That is fairly common. But there was a Hawaiian dude who worked in the factory and I think that he thought I needed a lesson in humility.

He put my name in big letters across the tail of the board, maybe three inches high. That was not what I had in mind but when I got the board there was no time to get it colored over.

That turned out to be not a problem. My board was stolen the first week. Then it showed back up a few days later with the name painted over. That was a clear message that I understood even clearer.

I got to surf in the Hawaii Junior Championship at Queens Surf that summer and took second place behind a great local surfer named Roland Sonata. Roland's brother Harry was a very talented local musician who I got to be good pals with. Also a couple other Waikiki kids about my age, Peter Pope and LeRoy Achoy. Both of those kids could shred.

* * *

By the end of that summer, my surfing had taken on a more complete approach.

When I got back to California I won the San Clemente contest again and right afterwards won the United States Championship in the Juniors as well as the paddleboard race. On top of that, I won the United States Surfing Association Championship at Salt Creek, which only had one division so I surfed against all the top men at the time.

That was the first year that Surfer Magazine held the SURFER POLL, where people vote for whom they feel are the twenty best surfers in the world. I got voted number 19 and was totally ecstatic.

I had told my dad that I was going to be a pro surfer and now I could see the light starting to brighten down the tunnel a little bit.

Corky Carroll – Not Done Yet

1963 Awards Ceremony for the Frst SURFER POLL.

Top row Left to Right: Joey Cabell, Greg Noll, Ricky Grigg, Phil Edwards, Paul Strauch, Mike Doyle, John Peck, Hobie Alter. Seated: Butch Van Artsdalen, Corky, Mickey Munoz, Pat Curren, L.J. Richards, Dewey Weber.

Photo: John Severson, SURFER Magazine.

* * *

In December of that year, I made my first trip to the North Shore of Oahu and got my first taste of the big waves. I went over with Mike Doyle, Mickey Munoz, Joey Cabell, and Chuck Linnen. A great lineup of top surfers, I was really lucky to be getting to tag along.

On the first day there we caught Sunset Beach pretty big. I was a lot more scared than I had anticipated.

These waves were A LOT bigger than they looked in the surf magazines. They were not only tall, but they were also massive in thickness and power.

It is like the whole ocean is moving around out there and you, as a mere human, are very powerless against all that energy.

After I took a few smaller ones I risked it and went for one of the bigger set waves. A great surfer from California named Kemp Aaberg took off in front of me. I knew that he knew what he was doing so I just followed him as close as I could without crashing into him. We both made the wave and the adrenalin rush was like nothing I had ever felt before. Kemp had a big smile on his face and said, "so you like this stuff huh?" I couldn't speak. I just let out a monster, "Awhooooooo!!!!"

Corky at Sunset Beach early 1960's.
Photo: LeRoy Grannis, courtesy of John Grannis

The next day the surf was even bigger and I got my first taste of Waimea Bay. This, along with Makaha, was the place where the biggest waves in the world were ridden at that time. Sunset Beach had been big and scary, but THIS was a whole different thing altogether. I had never felt so small and so insignificant as when I paddled out there the first time. Well, actually every time I paddled out there I always felt like that. Even years later when I had done it dozens of times. Surf that massive makes you realize that mama nature is in control and the best we can do is flow along with it, hope to take a thrill or two and get out alive.

As I am sitting there in a state of "why?," (as in "why did I do this?") I see George Downing also in the lineup waiting for a wave. He is looking at me with a kind of sly "knowing" grin on his face. I am wondering if he knows that I am peeing my pants in fright.

He says, "Hey Corky, you're pretty young to be out here. Are you scared?" I'm thinking sarcastically…. "Oh hell no George, I'm not scared at all. I do this every other day back home in front of my house in Surfside. Why would I be scared?"

What came out was a simple, and smallish, "yes."

George smiled and reassuringly said, "Good, then you will be O.K." I guess that was supposed to make me feel better. But I was still scared poopooless.

I rode three waves that day and didn't die. I was very happy when I got back to the beach too. I realized that it might be a good idea to learn how to hold my breath longer than the four seconds I could do in a warm bathtub. This stuff was serious. Most of the early big wave riders were also free divers and great swimmers who could hold their breath for weeks at a time. That was a huge advantage in giant surf. I could swim ok, but the holding my breath part would take some work.

Freddy Hemmings L, and Corky R, Waimea Bay 1963.
Photo: LeRoy Grannis, courtesy John Grannis

* * *

A few days later I got my first experience at the "Pipeline." This place had only just started to be ridden by guys on boards. From the first hairball drop, I fell in love with that wave. A screaming hollow sucking out left. It seemed all the good spots went right in those days. Being right foot forward I always had to be riding with my back to the wave. I like riding facing the wave better, most people do.

In later years I got to like going backside almost as much, but facing the wave gives you a certain visual perspective and ability to fit yourself inside a breaking wave better, especially back in those days when we were riding big heavy longboards. At least in my opinion, others may differ on that. And Pipeline was the perfect wave for fitting yourself deep into.

Corky at Banzai Pipeline, 1963.
Photo: LeRoy Grannis, courtesy of John Grannis

Pipe is one of the more dangerous surf spots in the world due to the shallow lava rock reef, probably more dangerous than Waimea Bay for that reason.

I never felt the same kind of fear at Pipeline. Respect yes, but I had much more confidence at that place than I did riding backside at Sunset Beach and Waimea Bay.

This was the beginning of a long love affair I had with that spot, one of my all-time favorite places to surf. In the early years I was able to catch it many times with almost nobody else, or nobody else, out. Then it became very crowded, but I still loved it anyway.

For my stay on the North Shore that winter I wound up living in an old Quonset hut out by a spot named "Velzyland." It was named after a great surfboard builder named Dale Velzy. I am not sure Velzy ever surfed there really.

What I am thinking is that one day there were a lot of guys out riding Velzy boards and somebody went, "geeze, what is this....Velzyland?" And the name stuck. That's just a guess, but it's my story and I am going with it.

Anyway, there were 15 guys, two dogs and one girl living in that old Quonset hut. All surf rats. Doyle, myself and Chuck Linnen were among them. Munoz and Joey had found someplace else to stay in town I think. We were on a full hardcore surf adventure while Mickey and Joey probably had other adventures in mind along with the surfing.

About a week or so into the trip everybody started noticing that they would have small bits of their food and drink missing.

The consensus was that it was Chuck Linnen who was sneaking bites and taking drinks. One day everybody got together and set a trap.

We took a milk carton that was nearly full and added some goodies to it. Nasty goodies. Without wanting to get real graphic and gross, I will just say that the least nasty of all the goodies would have been boogers.

After surfing that morning we pulled up in front of the house and started to unload the boards off the car. A few minutes later Chuck Linnen comes flying out of the house gagging and barfing up milk all over the place. It was such a wonderful moment.

We all cheered and laughed and chided him with rude and condemning remarks. The further punishment was that he was forced to buy everybody dinner that night at the Seaview Restaurant in Haleiwa. That probably took all his money so he was forced into sneaking more bites and drinks, but it was all forgiven in the long run.

* * *

That winter on the north shore was a real eye-opener for me as a surfer. I had never realized how much power there was in the big surf over there. Even on the smaller days, the waves had more speed and power than almost anything I had experienced in California before.

I loved the speed and from that winter on my approach to riding waves changed. I realized that everything is easier and more fluid when you have speed and power and I started to look for that in a wave. Going fast is a high and once you know how it feels you want it more and more.

This has stuck with my approach to surfing my whole life. I wanna go very fast because speed gives me freedom on a wave. Unfortunately, the boards we had back then were not exactly ready for real speed and one on one communication with the wave.

That would come a few years later.

Corky Carroll – Not Done Yet

The crew at the "barracks," Velzyland. North Shore - 1963.
Standing: Kemp Aaberg, unknown, Midget Farrelly, Candy Calhoun, Corky, Mike Doyle, Roy Crump. Sitting: Bob Bagley, unknown, Kent Casper.

CHAPTER 6

"Turning Pro"

As 1964 rolled around I was winning more and more contests in the Junior Men's Division and a couple in Open competition when there was no age grouping. I also had my first car, an old TR-10. This was a sort of squarish VW Bug like thing that was made by Triumph. I had racks on the roof for my board and was off every weekend to some sort of surf event or just on a surf trip somewhere up or down the coast. Being mobile was fantastic. It not only gave me the freedom to surf all kinds of surf spots that I had not been to before, it also allowed me to date chicks on a regular basis.

During the late winter and spring of '64, all kinds of things fell into place in my life.

Hobie had given me a job working in the surfboard factory late at night. My job was to take the fresh surfboard blanks before they were touched by the shapers and trim them down close to the thickness that the shapers needed them to do their work.

In those days the blanks came very thick and the wood stringers that were glued into them stuck out both sides. This was called "mowing down" the blank.

I was the chief blank mower downer and my hours were anytime I wanted to work between the time the shapers left for the day and when they showed up the next day. In other words, the middle of the night.

At about the same time I met "Banzai Betty." Banzai Betty was a very beautiful surf chick from Laguna Beach that was the girl featured in the Fender Guitar ads appearing in SURFER magazine.

She dazzled me.

She could surf and looked amazing with a perfect body and long brown hair. This was the perfect High School girlfriend for me and before long we hooked up. At that time it was called "going steady."

This was even a better situation when I moved into an apartment in Dana Point for the summer. I was not only close to work but also closer to Banzai Betty's house.

As fate would have it, one night after we had gone out to some sort of party or surf movie or something, I don't remember what it was, I went straight from the date to work in the surfboard factory. I was pretty tired but figured I would nail down a couple of hours before heading back to my apartment to catch some sleep.

When I was mowing blanks I always wore clear glasses to keep the wood chips and foam dust from getting into my eyes. Sometime during the night, I guess my glasses started to slip down my nose and I reached to adjust them with my right hand. I was holding the electric power plainer in my left hand at the time and it was in the locked-ON position.

Somehow I put my right arm right into the rotating blade on the power plainer and cut a huge hole in the inside of my arm, very close to the joint behind my elbow. Dark blood started squirting everywhere.

I totally panicked and tossed the power plainer onto a pile of foam dust and ran out the door, jumped into my car and floored it towards the Hospital in South Laguna Beach. I left the door open, all the lights on and the plainer still going in the pile of foam dust. And there was blood all over the room.

As it turned out I was lucky to have just missed the artery that is right there in that part of my arm, but still lost a lot of blood and would wind up with a large scar that is still on my arm today. It was a very close call.

The really amazing part of this whole ordeal was what happened the next day.

When the shapers started arriving for work the next morning the place looked like a murder scene. Blood all over the place and the lights still on, plainer still on and door wide open.

They all thought somebody came in and murdered me during the night and took away my body.

I was told that there was "mild concern" about me.

After everything that had happened that night I didn't rush right into the shop the next day to let everybody know I was O.K.

When I finally did I was told that "if I showed up, and was still alive, Hobie wanted to see me in his office." So, I went to talk to him that afternoon, expecting to be in trouble for leaving the shaping room in such a condition.

To my amazement Hobie was genuinely happy that I was not dead and didn't even chew me out for the mess.

What he did do was tell me that he had thought about it and realized that I had the potential to become a truly great surfer and was worth much more to him out surfing than stuck in a shaping room.

His feeling was I was better with a surfboard than with sharp objects. In fact, those were his very words, "you are much better with a surfboard than with sharp objects."

With that thought in mind he offered me the job of "paid professional surfer." He put me on salary to do nothing but surf and enter surfing contests.

His business manager, Jim Gilloon, was sitting there at that very moment and commented that this made me the world's first truly full- time professional surfer.

A few days later I was contacted by John Severson at *SURFER Magazine* with an offer from Jantzen Swimwear to become a part of their "International Sports Club" and appear in their advertising campaign.

Wow, just like that I had paid surfboard and swimwear endorsement deals in place.

I called up my dad and told him, "I did it pop!

I'm a PRO SURFER!!!"

CHAPTER 7

The Summer of... "The Endless Summer"

It's now the spring of 1964, I am 16 and happily basking in my new job as a pro surfer. I was living in the apartment in Dana Point with a couple of pals, including England born, Australian Rodney Sumpter, and enjoying a great romance with the lovely "Banzai Betty." Life is great.

Right about this time local surf movie maker Bruce Brown had just finished his epic film titled "The Endless Summer." It is based around a couple of guys who fly around the world chasing perfect surf and what you might consider a for real "endless summer."

When they were beginning to work on this film I was told my name was brought up as possibly being one of the two dudes to make the trip. But I was too young and it would have been too much trouble with borders, passports, etc. etc. etc.

Probably I was just too much of a brat. But hey.

One night Bruce invited the whole local surf crew over to his house to preview the film and make comments. It was, and still is, an amazing film. I loved it.

There was one shot of me in it at Malibu where my board rolled over and I bumped my head on the bottom as it did. When I came up Mickey Munoz was paddling out, and I was telling him that when my board rolled over I had hit my head.

Bruce Brown, always being one to make something funny and interesting out of nothing made a joke about it and called it my "El Rollo." It was in good humor, and I was just happy to be included in the movie.

A month later the movie was finished and plans were made for an eleven city East Coast Premier Tour. Hobie and Bruce had gotten together and arranged a combo surf movie and surfing exhibition trip from New York City to Miami.

They had gotten Ford Motor Company to let them use one of their new Ford Condors, the first of the new line of mobile homes that were self-driven, as opposed to house trailers. We affectionately, or not so much, called it "The Big Bird." They lined up Joey Cabell, Mike Hynson, myself, plus Phil Edwards and his wife Heidi to make the trip along with them and their wives. Nine of us in all.

Bruce held an invitation only premier of the movie in Santa Monica in early June, and right after that we pulled out of Dana Point one midnight headed across country for New York City. What a crazy trip that was.

At first everybody was all happy and stoked to be doing it. But after a few days and no privacy at all, along with the bathroom overflowing constantly due to Hobie's wife Sharon having to take constant showers, things got a bit tense.

I was the only one having fun. But I was also the only one 16 years old and on a great adventure.

The Endless Summer/Hobie promotional tour 1964.
Getting ready to leave Dana Point in the "Big Bird."
Photo courtesy of HOBIE Surfboards and Bruce Brown Films.

One night they let Mike Hynson drive and he got us lost. We wound up in some little town in Indiana called Hagerstown.

It happened to be the day of the annual Hagerstown Chicken Fry. At the same time of this trip, Hobie was just coming out with his first line of wood laminated skateboards with clay wheels.

We had a bunch of them with us and decided to make our entry into the chicken fry by skateboarding down a little hill from where we parked the Big Bird, basking in all its glory with a whole stack of surfboards tied on the roof.

To say the locals were surprised to see us would be a huge understatement. They were great and gave us all the chicken we could eat. The headline in the local paper the next day read *"Hawaiian Surfriders Invade Hagerstown Chicken Fry."*

It was the first time I felt a little bit of what it was like to be some sort of celebrity. We even signed autographs, another first for me.

But that was nothing compared to what was waiting for us along the East Coast.

We opened the tour with the first public showing of the movie in New York City followed by the surfing exhibition the next morning at Gilgo Beach. I was in shock when we pulled up and there were thousands of people waiting to see us. The surf was tiny, but it was a beautiful day.

Hobie parked the Big Bird at the top of the beach and Bruce got on the roof with the P.A. System he used for the movie and did running color commentary as we attempted to ride what waves that dared to roll in.

The biggest problem was that the crowd was so big that people waded out into the water to get a closer view. Some were actually standing right next to us as we were sitting on our boards waiting for waves and others were standing directly in the way, more or less of a hazard in the event we did catch a wave. Bruce had to try and keep them far enough away from us so we could surf, but it was a constant problem to keep them back and we almost ran down dozens of happy onlookers armed with cameras and white zinc oxide painted noses. It was a pretty amazing morning.

Bruce was happy, as the movie was a sellout and got rave reviews. Hobie was happy, as thousands of new surfers were born and running out to buy new Hobie boards from the newly set up Hobie dealer there.

As surfing was so new the Hobie dealer was actually a ski shop in Queens which semi converted to surfboards for spring and summer and then back to skis for fall and winter.

***

Also, while in New York I did an appearance on the "Tonight Show" with Johnny Carson. I was billed as the United States Junior Surfing Champion who was going to demonstrate the "new craze" of Skateboarding.

Hobie and his wife took me out and bought me a suit and a nice pair of shoes to wear on the show, which I thought was totally stupid as I was what I was, a surfer doing some skateboarding.

I would have been fine with shorts, t-shirt and barefoot. But they insisted that I should look good and like that was going to do it?

When I got to the show for rehearsal, and they asked me to show them what I was going to do, I found that the stage was extremely slippery. Just trying a simple turn I spun out and sent my board flying into the waiting audience who had already been seated. Nailed some poor dude in the third row right in the head, and they had to take him out for medical assistance.

So, for the actual show, they put sticky rosin down on the floor, which made it all gooey. After the spectator creaming in rehearsal Johnny had decided to NOT give it a try like had been planned and I decided to not try anything that might end in embarrassing disaster.

So, my big demonstration consisted of a couple of turns back and forth and that was it. I made it a point to say that this was the all-new "Hobie" skateboard, not Hobby. And I even spelled it out.

This made Hobie extremely happy and he told me later that I was becoming worth every penny he was paying me. I suggested he add a few pennies to that, but he just laughed and said, "keep it up and we will see."

The mid way spot on the tour was in Virginia Beach. The Hobie surfboard dealer there was an already established surf shop called "Smith and Holland."

It was named after the owners, Pete Smith and Bob Holland. This was the first time in weeks that we didn't have to sleep in the Big Bird. We were split up between Pete and Bob's houses.

Mike Hynson and I were put up at Pete Smiths while the rest of the crew stayed with Bob Holland, who had a big beautiful home a mile or so north of town.

As had to happen, the first night Mike and I went cruising the local hot spots and wound up meeting a couple of local chicks.

Mike took us back to Pete's house and I got the bright idea to take mine to the Big Bird. After all, it was empty and available. Mike bought us a six-pack and we walked up there about eleven o'clock in the evening. Small problem was the door was locked when we got there. So, I went around and found that the window on the driver's side was open. I got the chick to boost me up so I could crawl through the window and unlock the door.

There were visions of an extremely fun filled night running, no frolicking, through my head. But somehow I got stuck and sort of fell right onto the horn. It started blaring out and I couldn't seem to get myself free.

What I didn't know was that there were not enough bedrooms in Bob's house for everybody so Bruce and his wife Pat had decided to sleep in the Big Bird so they could be by themselves.

First time they had any privacy on the whole trip, and I guess they had just got to bed when I got stuck on the horn.

All the lights in the house came on and Bruce came out of the back in a rage. He pulled me off the horn, opened the door and punched me in the face as he tossed me out into a mud puddle. It had just started to rain.

The last I saw of my chick she was running down the street with our six-pack. That was the end of my fun night and the beginning of a long, long walk back to Pete's house in the rain.

The next day we had our exhibition and I showed up with a big black eye. Hobie took me aside and suggested that I just forget about it and not say anything to anybody about what had happened. I took his advice and just said my board hit me.

Bruce never said a word; in fact, he didn't really talk to me much at all after that. I did notice that his narration of my "el Rollo" in the movie started to take on a sort of sarcastic tone instead of the previous good-natured delivery that had been funny.

Hey, it wasn't like I knew they were in there. I thought they were in the house and we would have the Big Bird all to ourselves.

The Endless Summer Promotional Tour Crew
L to R - Mike Hynson, Bruce & Pat Brown, Joey Cabell, Corky, Hobie & Sharon Alter, Heidi & Phil Edwards
Photo: Courtesy of Hobie Surfboards & Bruce Brown Films

Simple mistake, but it kind of put an edge on what had been a nice friendship and I have had to live with his now sarcastic comment in the film ever since. Oh well, I wasn't going to let this affect the great time I was having on this trip nor the fact that I was just happy to be a part of the whole thing.

We ended the tour in Florida.

While there I met Gary Proper for the first time. Gary was my age and was the hottest surfer on the East Coast.

He came to surf with us one day and all of us were blown away at how well he could ride waves that were so small that we hardly even considered them rideable at all. He was a very animated and outgoing dude and I liked him right away. Hobie could see what great marketability he would have on the East Coast and I think arrangements were being made to bring him into the Hobie fold sooner or later.

* * *

Finally, we returned to Dana Point and I was able to actually get my real summer vacation underway. Unfortunately, or fortunately, as it might have been, my dad had crashed my car while I was gone. My dad was always a hard drinker and a heavy party dude.

Evidently he was at the Chart House in Newport Beach one night and somehow my car got totaled.

The upside was that he had replaced it with a 1957 Chevy Bel Aire Station Wagon. This was a much better surf mobile and more.

I decked the thing out with curtains in the back, a mattress, so I could sleep in it during surf trips up and down the coast, and very cool "vibrasonic" radio speakers to take the cool factor to another level.

The combination of Banzai Betty, that car, and me led to many extremely great adventures that year.

Another thing that happened during that summer was the beginning of my work with the Jantzen International Sports Club.

Corky Carroll – Not Done Yet

JANTZEN ad SURFER Magazine (back cover) vol. 9 no. 4 (September 1968). Corky appeared on every back cover of SURFER MAGAZINE for seven years in these iconic ads for Jantzen and was a member of its exclusive INTERNATIONAL SPORTS CLUB.

This was a small collection of guys from different sports that Jantzen had put together to use in the advertising for their men's line. It included basketball players Jerry West and Bob Cousy, football players Don Meredith, Frank Gifford, Timmy Brown, Lance Allworth and Paul Horning, a golf dude named Dave Marr and hockey star Bobby Hull.

Don Meredith and I became pals right off the bat, what a funny and cool dude. He was deep into country music and loved Willy Nelson. The fact that I knew that the country radio station in Los Angeles was KFOX told him that I was O.K. During photoshoots I always hung out with Don and had some great times.

I also became friends with Lakers star Jerry West. At the time I knew a little bit about pro basketball, but I can't say that I was all that deep into it. Jerry invited me to a game and I got to sit with his wife a few rows behind the Lakers bench.

Wow, that did it. I got totally hooked and to this day I am a die-hard purple and gold bleeding Lakers fan, and in fact write for one of the Lakers fan pages online. I am in heaven when they are winning and in agony when they aren't.

In the off-season, I follow all their trades and draft moves and everything else avidly. During the season I watch every game that I can that comes on television. Lakers are MY team.

I will never forget the morning that we found out Magic Johnson was going to have to retire due to having HIV.

We were doing a cruise for Miller Lite, more on that later, and we had just docked in Antiqua. I was walking down the hall on my way to the deck and somebodies' radio was on in a cabin and we heard something about President Bush and Magic Johnson and somebody had AIDS.

First thing out of my mouth was, "Oh God, I sure hope its Bush." This was obviously not because I wished any harm on the president.

I just didn't want it to be Magic. I love that dude. He is my all-time idol.

When he would come screaming down the court with that huge Cheshire cat smile on his face and have James Worthy on his left and Michael Cooper on his right you just knew it was lights out, one way or the other. The only question was just what unreal play he was gonna make, but for sure he was gonna make one.

I loved the "Showtime" Lakers era and would later do work with Worthy, Byron Scott, and Cooper at charity tennis events. Again, more on that later on.

Bobby Hull was another story. He was one of those dudes who have to prove to you how strong he is by breaking your hand when you meet him and go to do the handshake. He hurt me so badly the day we met that I never liked him a bit after that, he just always came off as a real mean and arrogant jerk in my eyes. I never have liked dudes who have to do that bone-breaking handshake thing, so probably I just didn't want to like him after that. I thought his kids were punks too.

The Jantzen connection was great for me and lasted until I retired from pro competition at the end of 1972. I think I was featured on the back cover of *SURFER Magazine* for something like six or seven straight years.

The head of the men's division was a super cool dude named Roger Yost. We are still in touch and remain pals to this day. I haven't seen either Don or Jerry in a number of years, although I did see Jerry at a Lakers game I went to with Jack Haley when his son was playing for the team during the 90's. I really wish Jerry was still working with the Lakers, the dude is a basketball genius.

* * *

There was a guy who lived down the street from us in Dana Point named "Tinker." He lived in a small pink house with John Severson's younger brother Joey, and they had a goat. The idea of that was so they would not have to mow the lawn.

Tinker was an interesting dude who seemed to be able to fix or make anything, hence the name "Tinker." His real name was Carl West but nobody knew that.

He was a glasser for Wardy Surfboards in Laguna Beach and drove this giant old panel truck, sometimes off-roading behind Dana Point in the hills on what he called "jungle cruises." I mistakenly went on one of those and up until that point in my life was the most scared I had ever been.

Tinker was also a musician. He used to sit around his living room playing and singing Bob Dylan songs on acoustic guitar, and with a harmonica on a rack. Listening to him sort of gave me the inspiration to maybe actually learn how to play an acoustic guitar. I would grab Joey's guitar and try to play along and that led me to try and learn some songs. But it would still be a little while before I fully committed to it.

* * *

When the summer of 1964 finally ended I moved back in with my parents in Surfside so I could keep going to Huntington Beach High School. It was the beginning of my senior year. Actually, at that time we were using the campus of the newly built Marina High as they were remodeling HBHS, but our class would graduate as HBHS class of '65. I never really got into the social scene at school due to the fact that most of my social activities took place in South County.

I would head down there after school on Fridays and spend the weekends there and return Sunday night to be ready for school on Mondays.

In December, I would make the trip back to the North Shore and also surf in the big Makaha International Championship. This was the year that my dad decided that he wanted to "go Hawaiian." Why I don't know. But he did and it was pretty strange for me.

It was not that I didn't want him along, but the fact that he was such a high-volume drinker and outrageous partier made it kind of awkward on me.

Mike Doyle and I went to the airport in Honolulu to pick him up the day he arrived and he was already totally wasted when he got off the plane.

He made his Hawaiian debut by falling down the stairs getting off the plane, jumping to his feet and grabbing the pilot by the hand and slobbering out, "Great driving pal."

When the chick was trying to put a lei around his neck I think he tried to hump her leg or something. All I know is she jumped back and screamed. This led the security guys to guide him off the runway and to make us promise to get him out of there immediately and sober him up.

We got him out of there ok, but he didn't sober up for the whole two weeks he was there. Sometimes he was really funny, other times I was totally embarrassed by the things he would do or say. He seemed to be having the time of his life nonetheless and I couldn't really fault him for that. He worked hard and he and my mom didn't get along very well at all.

He would come home half in the bag and my mom would get really pissed off about it and rag him so bad that he would stomp off to bed. They had separate rooms. This was pretty much a nightly thing.

So, I guess this trip was some kind of release for him and he took full advantage of it to just let go and rage. Which he did, in full glory and living color.

I had always been close with both my parents even when they were fighting. This trip to Hawaii more or less began a slow decline in how close I was with my dad though. Even though I was glad he was having a good time it was still hard to be around him, or anybody for that matter, when he was fully drunk to the max all the time. He would get up and have a couple of martinis and wash them down with a beer just to get himself going.

I started sneaking off to surf when he wasn't paying attention just so I could be away from him for a while. I began to fully understand what my mom was dealing with and why she got so angry with him all the time. Fun is fun, but this was kinda ugly. Oh well, it just was what it was.

We were all staying in a house out by Velzyland that surf movie-maker Dale Davis had rented. I really liked Dale a lot.

Mike and I did a lot of surfing together for Dale's upcoming movie and I think it was really that winter that I became to fully appreciate the amazing surfing skills that Mike had in big surf, and just how far ahead of most anybody else he was in massive conditions.

I would see him make free falling late takeoffs at Waimea Bay on giant days when I was in fear for my life and being as ultra-careful as possible. He would pull big bottom turns and get really deep.

I don't think the published versions of surfing history gave Mike the credit he truly deserves as one of the greatest surfers of all time, he truly was.

* * *

One last note on 1964, is that it was the year I learned the hard way about the media. I was asked to do an interview for Surf Guide Magazine, and I was very excited about it.

This took place early in the year before the Endless Summer trip. They sent a guy named Bill Cleary down to our house in Surfside to interview me. I didn't know him, and he didn't know me, but I guess he had some sort of preconceived ideas about me.

I had no idea what to say and honestly, he had no idea about what to ask me. He pretty much only did the basic stuff like "who influenced you the most" and that was about it.

He said he had all he needed and would put "a great story together." He also said he would send it to me for my approval before it went to print. Well, neither of those ever happened.

The story came out headlined as "Corky the Clown." He made up pretty much the whole thing only using some of what I had said, mostly twisting words to sound the way he wanted them to sound. The "Clown" part didn't really bother me so much as I have always had a sense of humor and liked to joke and clown around.

Unfortunately for me, during my life, many people either did not get the joke or understand that I was actually trying to be funny, and they took it seriously.

Well anyway, this dude definitely put a weird slant on the story and I felt it was pretty embarrassing.

I talked to Hobie about it and his take was that anybody who knew me would be fine with it but in the future, I had better be more careful with the press.

Obviously I didn't learn that lesson right off the bat and went on to make many such blunders as time went on.

My attitude was "well if they can't take a joke…" That attitude got in the way of probably many friendships that I never got to have. I thought I was totally cool, but there were many who totally didn't.

* * *

It was about that time when I started hanging out with a really good surfer from Laguna Beach that was my age, Billy Hamilton. Billy and I had sort of opposite directions on how we were developing our surfing skills.

He was super smooth and spent hours looking at photos of guys like Skip Frye and Phil Edwards to make sure he knew exactly how to place his hands and even his fingers. At first, he didn't have any really big moves, but he looked amazing doing what he did have.

I was still more all over the place as far as having perfect hand and finger placement went. Eventually, both of us would round into complete surfers, but at first, we were just two gremmies who were stoked to the max and lived and breathed surfing. We went to a lot of the contests together, sometimes with Mark Martinson along too. Plus, we surfed together at Cotton's point, Trestles, Salt Creek and Doheny all the time.

I remember one time we drove up to Santa Barbara to surf the Hollister Ranch. We had no way to get in, so we decided to walk.

One day we walked in from the North, probably six miles each way. The next we walked in from the South, calling it 3 or 4 miles each way.

Both days the surf was tiny and the walk was totally miserable each way. But we didn't care at all, it was an adventure. Billy has always been one of my favorite people in surfing and a guy who I respect as one of the greatest surfers I have ever seen. He certainly has the best style that I know of. His stepson is the famous big wave waterman Laird Hamilton.

CHAPTER 8

"The Brave New World"

In June 1965 I graduated from Huntington Beach High School and moved out of my parents' home for good.

I had rented a little cottage in Dana Point that was just perfect for myself and my dog "Boris." Boris was a springer spaniel that was a great dog but not the prettiest in the world. It had actually been my dad who gave him the name Boris, after the not so pretty horror movie actor Boris Karloff.

I was living off of my weekly salary from Hobie to surf, and my Jantzen retainer. Sometimes money would be thin though, supporting myself full time and spending most of the time driving all over the coast surfing and promoting the boards, took every cent I was making.

I can vividly remember one time when I was totally out of money and there was no food in the house. It was a Thursday night and payday was on Friday. The only thing there was to eat was my dog Boris's very last Gainsburger.

Corky Carroll – Note Done Yet

For those of you who don't know what that is, it was a dog food patty that they used to sell which was basically just normal dog food shaped into a burger like form.

Boris was hungry and so was I. The only thing to do was fry that sucker up and split it with him. I put salt and pepper and the last of the ketchup on my half. Tasted just like what it was, dog food. I tried to tell myself it was just bad corn beef hash. But no, it was dog food.

* * *

That summer Tom Morey put on the very first professional surfing contest, actually offering a cash prize for the first time in surfing history. It was the Tom Morey Noseriding Invitational. The premise was that it would be a timed noseriding event. The guy who rode the most time on the nose, considered the first 25% of the board, would win. They held it at California Street in Ventura, which was a right- hand point break.

To make things fair they had both regular foot and goofy foot divisions. Invitations were sent to the leading surfboard manufactures who would be allowed to enter two of their team riders.

Tom's objective here was to stimulate surfboard design. As noseriding was the big deal at that time he figured a timed noseriding event would push the surfboard makers into coming up with new and better designs of boards to ride the nose. And it worked.

The design trio of Hobie Alter, Phil Edwards and Mickey Munoz successfully came up with the concept for the "noserider" shape that is still in use today. Concave under the nose, a very straight rocker with some lift in the tail. They added a very heavy fin to add drag so the board would slow down allowing the rider to stay on the nose longer.

The Hobie factory team was Mickey Munoz in the regular foot division and me in the goofy-foot division, and we both won. The cash prize was a whopping 250 bucks each.

Corky on the original HOBIE noserider design board, Poche 1965.
Photo: Ron Stoner - Courtesy of HOBIE Surfboards.

Aside from our Hobie noseriders there were some interesting and pretty unusual boards that turned up. The only ones close to what we had were the Gordon and Smith team of Mike Hynson and Skip Frye. Mike had made a couple of nice boards with wide noses and flat bottoms. Good, but ours were better.

Rusty Miller had a board with two bricks glued to the tail and Dewey Weber had two pontoon kinda thingies glued under the nose.

The classic entry was Mike Doyle's. He had made a board that was 10' long. However, it had a stringer that stuck out the back for an additional 10'.

Thus, he claimed, his board was actually 20' long and therefore the first half of the surfboard itself would be considered the nose.

Obviously this was what you would call a "rule beater." Tom Morey figured this was "not in the spirit" of the contest and would not let Mike get away with it. He could ride the board but only the first 25% would be considered the nose. Mike, not all that happy with this revolting development, decided to split and not surf in the contest.

After that event, I decided maybe it was time for me to get out of the junior's division in the contests.

I had just won the Noseriding contest and had already won the USSA championship previously at Salt Creek surfing against the men.

So, even though I was still 17, I switched in midyear to the open men's division and won the first two events I surfed in. I guess it was the right decision.

At the same time, Hobie had decided to release both Corky Carroll and Gary Proper signature model boards.

The idea was mine would be designed for West Coast and Hawaii surf and Gary's would be for the East Coast.

I was both happy, and not so much about this. I was happy because this would be a big bump in my income. But not so much because the majority of surfboard sales were on the East Coast at that time, in fact still are.

Hobie assured me that they would sell mine back there too, and it was just a good way for him to cover the market as well as possible.

In any case, this was a good thing and I was stoked.

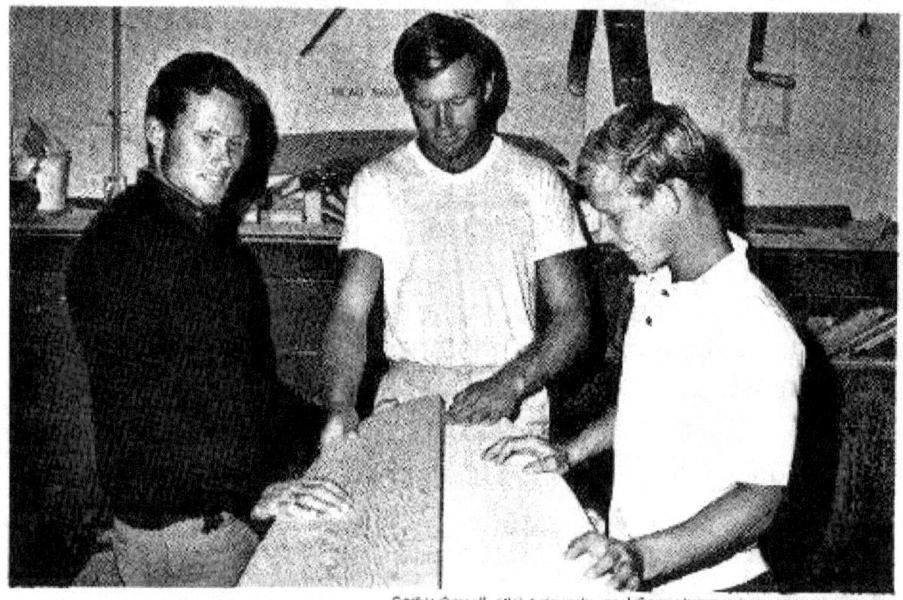

Hobie Ad; Corky, Phil Edwards and Gary Propper

Winners of the Oceanside Invitational 1965.
Pete Peterson and his tandem partner Sharon Barker (Groves),
Corky, Mike Doyle and Joyce Hoffman .
Photo: LeRoy Grannis, courtesy of John Grannis

* * *

Things were starting to come together as far as this being a pro surfer thing went and I was embarking on a really good run.

This was all new territory and with each little addition to ways to make this work, it was breaking new ground.

It truly was, as far as professional surfing went, a brave new world.

Corky Carroll – Note Done Yet

Corky was winning most of the surfing events held in the beach breaks of Southern California in the 1960's.
Photo from the Carlsbad Championship held at "Tamarack" 1965 by LeRoy Grannis, courtesy of John Grannis.

At the beginning of summer, about a week after I graduated from High School, my parents' house in Surfside burnt down.

I was living in Dana Point on my own full time now and read about it in the paper. I rushed up there to find my dad shifting through the ashes looking for anything he could salvage.

His first words to me when he saw me arrive where, "Sorry kid, all your trophies are gone." Geeze, like THAT mattered. Everything was gone. But he was always so proud of me and in his mind the fact that he lost some of my trophies was important to him. I was much more concerned about the fact that this was their home and now it was gone.

In the long run, I think this is what started the beginning of the end of my parents' marriage.

My mom had been in the bathtub when the fire started next door and she barely got out of the house before it totally went up. She was very nervous anyway and this shook her to the core. Probably made my dad drink more too. Bad combination. They wound up renting a house down the way a little bit in Sunset Beach, but I don't think things were really ever the same for them.

* * *

As I was totally on my own now and starting to have a little bit more money in my pocket, it became easier for me to travel around more.

In the winter I would go to Hawaii and started a love affair with "Pipeline" (the surf spot) that lasted for over thirty years. The last time I rode it was on my 50th birthday, I will get to that story later.

It was on one sort of last-minute trip over there to catch a really good swell that I first really hurt my back.

Pipe was really good and back then unless it was during December when everybody was over there, hardly anybody surfed there.

I had it almost to myself for three solid days in late October.

On the third afternoon, I was out with just one other guy, a really good surfer named Mike Turkington, when I took a very bad wipeout and got rammed into the bottom sitting down. I had a huge pain in my back and crawled up on the beach and burrowed into some warm sand to try and make it feel better.

It didn't and I could not sleep that night. The next day I flew back to California and saw my doctor. He said it was probably a "sprain" and to take it easy and it would go away. So I did and it got better but never did really go away. At times it would get sore and make it hard to surf, but it never got to the point where I felt I couldn't surf or couldn't deal with stuff. Nonetheless, it was always there and always something I had to be careful about.

* * *

Along with being able to go back and forth to Hawaii pretty much as I pleased, I was also able to go skiing all I wanted. And I loved to ski almost as much as I loved to surf.

I began going up to Mammoth Mountain, which was about an 8 hour drive from my house. Sometimes I would surf in a contest on the weekend, drive to Mammoth on Sunday night, ski Monday to Thursday, drive home Friday and surf another contest the next weekend. This wasn't an every week thing, but it did happen a number of times.

Starting that year I was able to get in at least sixty days of skiing every year along with surfing in just about every event that came along, not only in California but all over the place.

Competitors area for the Duke Kahanamoku Invitational held at Sunset Beach, December 1965. Sitting left to right: Fred Hemmings, Paul Strauch, Eddie Aikau, Ricky Grigg, Corky, Greg Noll, unknown, Mike Doyle kneeling.

Photo: Tim McCullough

* * *

That December they held the first DUKE KAHANAMOKU INVITATIONAL in Hawaii. The top 24 surfers in the world were invited to compete and the invitation included airfare, meals, and rooms at one of the top hotels in Waikiki. Each surfer was also given a bag of clothes and a beautiful gold trophy, which was a statue of Duke that looked like an Oscar, for competing. Having one of those "Dukes" was a very cool thing. I think I wound up with seven ofthem in all, and they were extremely special to me.

They held the contest on a good day in big surf at Sunset Beach on the North Shore.

I made the finals, which, for me, was a huge success. Jeff Hackman, who was another kid my age and lived on the North Shore, won it. Jeff was an amazing surfer and really cool guy. I had become friends with him and another kid who lived out there named Jock Sutherland. We were all the same age and all up and coming "gremmies."

I would have liked to have won, but it was really great seeing Jeff get it. Just making the finals made me feel good and I think showed people that I was not just a small wave California guy that could only go left in beach breaks. Some people probably thought that. I could also ride big waves and could go both ways as well.

Corky surfing in the finals of the first Duke Kahanamoku Invitational, Sunset Beach, HI. Photo: Tim McCullough

CHAPTER 9

"The Beginning of the Big Change"

1966 would be the real beginning to my best years as far as being a competitive professional surfer. I won a ton of events that year including the Men's division, paddleboard race and Duke Kahanamoku trophy for "Best Around Surfer" at the United States Championship. Things were picking up all the way around.

I do want to mention something here though that is noteworthy. When we were sitting on the beach, waiting for our final heat to go out at the U.S. Championship, the six of us finalists were watching the junior division. David Nuuhiwa was in it and probably turned in the best performance of his competitive life. There are many photos documenting him perched on the nose doing a killer "soul arch." It seemed that all of us sort of in unison went, "wow, glad he is still in the juniors."

This is important for a number of reasons. David was without a doubt the best noserider of that period. I don't think anybody would argue that. He had a beautiful smooth style, and he would just get up there and stay and stay. At that time in the United States noseriding was a really big deal, and he was the king of the noseriders.

Corky Carroll – Note Done Yet

Corky being interviewed at the Laguna Masters Championship by Wide World of Sports, Redondo Beach 1966.
Photo: LeRoy Grannis, courtesy of John Grannis

UNITED STATES SURFING CHAMPIONSHIP 1966,
Huntington Beach, Ca.
Left to right: Joey Cabell 6th, L.J. Richards 4th, Donald Takayama 2nd, Corky (winner), John Peck 3rd , Mike Doyle 5th.
Photo: LeRoy Grannis, courtesy John Grannis.

* * *

Shortly after the U.S. Championship, they held the World Championship in San Diego. The top surfers from everywhere were coming to compete.

Just before the contest was supposed to start we started hearing rumors about a guy from Australia named Nat Young who had been surfing the previous week up north of Santa Barbara. He was reported to be riding some new kind of board and was really looking good.

When we checked in for the contest they made us produce the boards that we would be riding in the event and were told that we could not change during the weeklong event.

This was a first, had never happened before. I guess the Australians were sure that when we saw Nat riding whatever it was he was going to ride that we would all go out and make new boards overnight.

Which, knowing what we know now, actually could have happened. The truth was that Nat's board was not all that different than ours, it was just shorter. Not a lot shorter, but shorter enough to make a remarkable difference in performance. His turns were quicker and his overall performance on the wave was, well the best way to say it, "overall" better. We could see this right off the bat as the competition got under way.

This event was going to actually be three contests and one final heat at the end.

On the first day I beat Nat in the semi-finals, but he came back thru a loser's heat to make the final. David was on fire and got the longest noseride on record to that time. I started off good but got caught inside for most of the heat. David won, Nat second, Jock Sutherland third and me forth.

After that first day David would wind up losing early and Nat didn't lose again. By the time the last day came around for the ultimate final heat at Ocean Beach Nat had so many points that he already had the title won. Jock would wind up in second place and me in third.

That was a huge day for surfing as, at least in my mind, it was the very beginning of the monumental change that would be ultimately called the "shortboard revolution."

Many people have different versions on this, but I'll give Nat Young total credit for starting this big change right then and there in October 1966.

Corky Carroll – Note Done Yet

Corky with Duke Kahanamoku, winning the DUKE award for "Best All Around Surfer" at the U.S. Championship in 1967. It was the second time in Corky's incredible string of winning the award, 5 years in a row - 1966, 67, 68, 69 and 70.
Photo: LeRoy Grannis, courtesy of John Grannis

Corky Carroll – Note Done Yet

Corky in the finals of the World Championship at Ocean Beach in 1966.

Photo: LeRoy Grannis, courtesy of John Grannis

***

That was also the year that I was starting to make a little bit of money. I was thinking that I should invest in something or maybe buy a house. The house idea seemed to be the best bet, but there was the problem that I was only 18. So, I went to my parents and told them I wanted to buy a home and if I put up all the money could they take out the loan in their name, and when I turned 21 and had established good credit we could get it transferred into my name. They thought it was a great idea and agreed.

My mom helped me shop, as she was a dedicated real estate looky-loo, and one of her favorite things to do was look at property, even if she had no intention whatsoever to buy anything. She just loved to look at stuff.

We found a nice little duplex in Capistrano Beach. This was ideal because I could live in one unit and rent out the other to help with the monthly house payment, taxes and insurance.

I put in the down payment and my dad got a loan for the financing. I would pay him the payment each month, which included taxes and property insurance.

How cool that was, I was 18 and a homeowner.

CHAPTER 10

"The Evolution" ~ 1966 – 1967

After the World Contest in San Diego I went on a sort of binge experimenting period, trying to come up with a direction for shorter boards.

Hobie was amazing with me and gave me a free hand to have as many boards made as I wanted. In the quest to come up with a not only workable but, also a sellable design for the next step in my surfboard model line.

I had been working with very thin and flexible boards up until this point. However, I totally gave up on that idea when it became clear to me that the direction should be shorter. Thin did not work so well with the first shorter boards because we were also trying to keep as much floatation as possible as we were taking away length. I tried a slew of different shapes and took a little of this and a little of that and came out with the Mini Model in December 1966.

The first incarnation of this board came mostly in 7'11" to 8'11" lengths. They also more or less resembled a longboard that was just shorter. For that time period, they were pretty radical and allowed me to surf in a completely different manner than I had been doing only a couple of months previously. It seemed, at least in my mind, that every day I went surfing was a whole new experience, and I was able to break new ground almost wave to wave. It was such a truly exciting time and I just got engulfed in it.

Corky Carroll – Note Done Yet

Summer 1966 issue of COMPETITION SURF with Corky on theCover.

***

1967 started off great for me. I went to Peru and won the International Big Wave Championship at Punta Rocas, being the first to dethrone local Felipe Pomar at his home break.

I also got incredibly sick while down there and spent a week in the hospital trying to recover, just before the final heat of the Championship.

I had flown down there with the infamous Mickey Dora, Malibu's "Black Knight" of surfing, and he came to visit me in the hospital.

Word was that they were not going to release me in time for the finals of the Championship; I was still very weak and not taking solid food yet.

I asked Mickey to help me escape, as I had not come this far and made it all the way to the finals to let myself get stuck in the hospital and miss it.

So, Mickey came up with a plan where he would engage the doctor in discussion in the hallway while I slipped out the door and jumped into the elevator that was right next to my room. The car was just outside the front door on the street. This was in downtown Lima.

Sounded like a good plan.

First snag was I had no clothes there; I had been taken to the hospital in an ambulance after having been found passed out on the floor of the bathroom in the home I was staying in. All I had was the hospital gown I was wearing, and it only came to my waist.

So, for all intents and purposes, I was naked from the waist down.

Nonetheless, I went with the plan and when Mickey had the doctor engaged, with his back to the door of my room, I snuck out and jumped into the elevator and headed down.

Second snag was this was not the normal elevator, it was a service elevator. When it opened I was in the kitchen. There were nurses and cooks and workers all over the place and there I was running out of the elevator looking for a way out.

Everybody was just staring at me with wide eyes. I saw an open window across the room and went for it. How I made a perfect dive through that thing I don't know, but I did. Would have gotten a 10 in the diving out the window Olympics.

Did I mention that I had no idea what was outside the window or even if I was on ground level?

Lucky for me I landed in a little grass strip that was next to the sidewalk. Mickey was coming out the front door, which was about 50 yards away, and pointing towards the car. He opened the back door and I ran and jumped in just as our driver, one of the local surfers, screeched outta there.

People on the street were in a state of shock as this half naked gringo dude went streaking by and leaping into a getaway car. You could not script this stuff.

The capper was that I won the contest the next morning.

The hospital had actually sent the police to arrest me for leaving without paying my bill, but thankfully our Peruvian hosts settled up on that, and I was not taken to jail.

The surf was pretty big, and they gave us an hour for the final heat. Best five rides would count for your total score.

I was not feeling great and I paddled out far and just waited for the biggest sets. I caught a total of six waves, all of them big, long and high scoring.

From what I understand the Peruvian contest officials were not real happy as I was the first one to beat the local defending champion, the great big wave rider Felipe Pomar. But even so they were very gracious, and I got a big ol' gold and silver trophy.

Corky winning the International Big Wave Championship at Punta Rocas, Peru in 1967.
Felipe Pomar 2nd, Corky Winner, and Jock Sutherland 3rd.

* * *

Following that adventure, I went to Florida for what was billed as the World Small Wave Championship. I was now riding the new "mini model" full time and was the only one riding shorter boards in just about every event that entire year.

I had a very hard time convincing anybody that this was the way to go. Surf shop owners did not want to stock them and most of the other competitors thought they were better off staying on their longboards. The catch was that I was winning almost all the events, including that one in Florida. Some of the shops would order mini models that were like 9'6" long and weren't mini at all, just longboards with mini model stickers on them. It was a hard sell.

One of my favorite memories of this period was when I went to Hawaii with a small quiver of mini-models, from 8'2" to 8'11" that ran from small wave to mini-gun. When I ran into infamous surfboard designer guru Dick Brewer. His matter of fact quote was "they will NEVER ride shortboards in Hawaii, PERIOD."

Much later he made an 8'11" semi-gun for Gary Chapman and to this day claims that was the first mini-gun, and he and he alone invented the shortboard.

I love that. Now, I am not saying that I, and I alone did. In my mind it was an evolution that took place over a few years and many hands were involved in it, but I am saying it's pretty funny that Dick takes credit for this when like a year before he made one himself, he told me beyond a shadow of a doubt that they would NEVER ride shortboards in Hawaii.

This is meaning no disrespect to Dick, he is a great and legendary shaper and designer, some of my best big wave boards ever where shaped by him when he worked for Hobie, but it is just an example of the uphill battle I was going through in order to get the surfing world to get on board with under nine-foot lengths during that first year.

I would wind up winning the United States Championship again, then traveling to Puerto Rico to win the Puerto Rico International and finally finished off the year by winning the first International Professional Championship in big surf at Steamers Lane in Santa Cruz.

That was one of the best years I had competitively speaking and by the end of the year people were finally starting to open their eyes and minds to the fact that maybe this shortboard thing was really going to happen.

Corky Carroll – Note Done Yet

Corky winning U.S. Championship at Huntington Beach in 1967.
Left to right: Duke Kahanamoku (seated), Mike Purpus 6th, Herbie Fletcher 4th, Donald Takayama 2nd, Corky - Winner, Skip Frye 3rd, Steve Bigler 5th

Photo: LeRoy Grannis, courtesy John Grannis

Corky with first place trophy, U.S. Championship 1967.
Photo: LeRoy Grannis, courtesy John Grannis

***

Another good thing that happened to me in November 1967 was getting married to a great girl named Cheryl Hendrix.

Cheryl had moved to San Clemente from Hollywood, and we had been dating for most of the year.

She was very pretty with long brown hair and brown eyes and is to this day, one of the best people I have ever known, and truly is one of those with, a "heart of gold."

During the summer we made a trip to Oregon together, where I surfed in the Oregon State Championship at a place called "Otter Rock." It was probably on that trip that things really jelled between us and led to us getting married.

It was also part of a growing thing with me surfing in that part of the world. I had been up there previously for a Jantzen convention held in Portland.

On a free day, I hired a taxi driver to take me to the coast, so I could see if there was any surf up there. To my amazement, I found great waves and a perfect left point.

From that time thru the early to mid-1970s I spent a couple of weeks a year in the fall surfing all over the Oregon coast, but mostly around Seaside where that left point is. In the beginning, I would be the only person out. Then local guys started surfing more and others moved up from Santa Cruz and other areas of California. By the early 1970s it was getting "localized."

The last time I went was during the years I was living in Sun Valley, Idaho (more on that later) and it was the closest surfing spot. Always loved it up there, the combination of mountainesque scenery with surf and ocean is alluring to me.

Although now, as I am writing this, I would never be able to deal with the cold like I could back then. Let's face it; it is really cold up there.

It was around this time, when I was on one of my surf trips up there, that I found a really cool house for sale in a little cove that had a surf spot out front. There was a big rock with a left going off one side of it and a right on the other. It was a big 5-bedroom New England style place that came with like a half-acre of land on a little knoll above the beach. The price was about $10,000. At that time this was a considerable amount of money, but I found myself thinking of how I might be able to buy it.

It was around then, a dude named Jim Jenks was trying to raise money to start a surfwear company that he was going to call Ocean Pacific. Jim went to a number of people in the Dana Point area who might have money to invest and offered 9.9% ownership of his new company for an investment of $10,000.

There was that number again. The funny thing was I had almost exactly that in my savings account. This was a really hard decision to make, buy the really cool beach house in Oregon or invest in Ocean Pacific.

I wasn't really sure that Jim was going to be able to pull off the surfwear thing, and I also thought that it should have been called Ocean Atlantic because the majority of the surfing business was on the East Coast.

So, I mulled it over and over in my mind and did exactly what any 19-year-old surf and fun crazed dude would do. I bought a brand new 911 Porsche. Hell yes, was there really any other choice?

Did O.P. go on to become one of the most successful and profitable surfing businesses in history?

Well, yes. Did the house in Oregon wind up being worth a couple million? Well, yeah there is that too. Do I still have the Porsche? Well, no.

Did it cost me a fortune in speeding tickets and insurance plus sky-high maintenance costs? Uh, yeah, that too. Did I ever regret this choice? Sometimes a little bit yes, but not anymore.

***

I loved my life right at this minute, and if I had not done things the way that I did them then, I might not be where I am now doing what I am doing, so in that regard, I don't regret those decisions, as stupid as they were at the time.

Hobie bought the share offered to both him and to me. In later years when I was struggling to find a way to survive, mentioned the multi-millions he had made from that investment in O.P.

I asked him if I could have some, thinking it only fair. He smiled big and just said, "nope." Oh well.

In November, they held the first International Pro-Am at Steamers Lane in Santa Cruz. There would be a cash prize for the Pro Division. The surf was big, and I was the only one riding a shortboard in the finals.

Although this was common for me that year, this was probably the last time that this happened. In any case, I had a very good day and took home the winner's check for a whopping $400 bucks as I remember.

***

After coming back from Hawaii that December Cheryl and I decided to spend the rest of the winter in Puerto Rico. I had liked it when I went there for the International Championships.

When they had announced that the World Championship would be held there in that next fall, we had just found out that Cheryl was pregnant too, so thought it would be a great getaway before the baby was born.

We arrived in early January 1968 and wound up renting a little concrete house on a hill overlooking the beach.

An amazing coincidence was that my pal Tom Morey, same as the noseriding contest Tom Morey, had just gotten there and was living right next door with his wife.

It was a great bit of luck as the four of us had a wonderful few months hanging out. We surfed and talked story and all kinds of weird theory stuff that Tom would come up with. He is like surfing's mad scientist.

I had taken 4 boards with me, one of which was a swallowtail with set up for three fins, one in the middle and two on the outside. This way it could be ridden as either a single fin, a twin fin or a tri fin.

The big problem was that this was in the time of big heavy fins.

This board had three fin boxes that were also heavy.

So, even though it was way ahead of its time, design-wise, it still was not really that functional as all the weight from the extra fins and boxes made it so tail heavy that it just didn't work very well at all.

It did stimulate a ton of discussion between Tom and me about multi-fin boards and just about every other kind of cosmic idea we could come up with.

I didn't understand much of it to tell you the truth, Tom's mind thought in much farther out spheres than mine. I just knew how to ride the things and had some ideas on what made them work.

Meanwhile, Tom is relating the whole thing to space travel and spiritual levitation.

My most productive contribution to most of the conversations was the occasional "wow." But then, "wow" was a big word in the late 60s, used for all sorts of things. So actually it went a long way.

When the surf was flat, and we weren't in some deep cosmic conversation, the two of us would go spear diving to score fish for dinner.

We had bought a couple of spear guns from a local dive shop. The deal was that whoever speared the first fish didn't have to hold the bag.

Unfortunately for me, Tom was a much better shot than I was so pretty much every time I would wind up holding the bag.

On one of those days, when I was on bag duty, we had nailed quite a few fish and the bag got filled up.

As we were close to shore and were diving right on the reef at a spot named "Marias," which was where we surfed most of the time, I decided to swim in and empty the bag, so we could get a few more.

As I was cruising in over the shallow reef I came to a spot where there was a break and I could see the sand about ten feet deep. All of a sudden a huge fish came swimming out from under the reef. "WOW," I thought. (see, there is that "wow" again, just like that) There was no way I could miss that sucker. I decided to swim down and spear that dude, figuring that if I brought in this fish beast I would never have to hold the bag again.

Great plan. Until just before I was going to pull the trigger and it spread out.

Yeah, I said, "spread out." It wasn't a big fish after all, it was a GINORMOUS octopus.

I mean we are talkin' Captain Nemo stuff here folks, release the Kraken. Holy freaking moly!!!

Forget the big waves, this was one of the most terrified I have ever been in my life. All I remember is looking into that big eye and knowing I had to get out of there immediately.

I launched out of the water and ran to the beach on the tips of my fins. I know I went in right over the reef and had the cuts to prove it.

I was huddled in the sand shaking. Cheryl was trying to figure out what was the matter with me. I was just pointing to the water and muttering, "M ma ma monster!"

It was at this point in my life that I came to the revolution that it is definitely not a good idea to dive where you surf.

You wind up knowing way too much about what is under you. And this point was further driven home in my little surf-soaked brain a couple of weeks later.

One of the really cool things about that winter in Puerto Rico was that there were almost no other surfers around most of the time. On the weekends a few would come out from San Juan, but other than that it was just us and a guy from the East Coast named Wayne Williams, who was camping by Maria's, and a couple of locals.

Tom and I spent many days checking out all the surf spots on that end of the island. One day we had driven to a very remote beach called Playa Jobos. It was pretty far from anywhere and was one of the most beautiful little places I had ever seen. Like a palm treed paradise with a little beach and very nice peaks breaking outside.

On this particular day, it was about four to five feet and very good. We were sitting out there trading waves and probably talking about something cosmic when, far off in the distance, we spotted these two fish skipping on top of the water and coming in our direction. One fish was about two feet long and just behind him was a fish about four feet long. Obviously the one in the front was trying to get away from the one in the back. There were just skipping across the water going really fast.

The one in the front was just trying to keep its tail away from the open mouth of the one behind. They went right by us going really fast and off into the distance as far as we could see.

Finally, and I should have known better, I asked Tom if the little fish was gonna get away or would the big fish wind up eating him. Tom did the classic chin rub and "hmmm" thing, and then calmly proclaimed the big fish would wind up eating the smaller fish. Sadly, I asked why. He explained, in his perfect surf scientist manner, that the little fish was using up more energy than the big fish because he was smaller. Therefore, he would wear out faster and when he did the big fish would have him for lunch.

I thought about this for a few moments and said, "Wow, that is really kinda sad." To which Tom point blankly said, "Well kid, that's life in the food chain!" "The FOOD CHAIN? Oh man, I don't like the food chain." I will never forget that.

Put this little lesson together with the encounter with the Moby Dick of Octopus's and my "in the water comfort zone" had been greatly compromised.

On land people are pretty safe and secure, I guess unless you live in an African jungle or something.

Set foot in the water, and we become part of this dreaded food chain thing, and we are not all that high in the chain either. After that winter I have never gone spearfishing again.

It was a nice time down there though, and we surfed a ton of good uncrowded waves. I got to know the spot where they were scheduled to hold the upcoming World Championships the next fall very well and was feeling I would have a good chance to win the title.

Corky at Domes - Rincon, Puerto Rico. World Championship 1968.
Photo: LeRoy Grannis, courtesy John Grannis

CHAPTER 11

"Prime Time"

Returning to California things really started to heat up for me. I was named as the "Top Surfer in the World" by SURFER Magazine's reader poll and was featured on their first-ever fold-out cover.

With the shorter boards really starting to catch on, Hobie was selling tons of my designs. We had modified the "mini-model" a bit and the sizes were getting shorter, so we renamed it the "super-mini." Hobie would wind up selling over 3000 Corky models that year which would heavily contribute to the best year financially that I had as a competitive professional surfer.

Things were going really well and in June my oldest son Clint was born. Being a parent is pretty "grounding." I was very happy.

Big summer issue of SURFER Magazine 1968.
First issue with a fold out cover, and Corky on three out of four of them. He won the SURFER Poll Award and had a photo of surfing at Cotton's Point. It was also the first time the magazine put a photo of a person's face on the front cover.

* * *

In the spring I did a trip up the East Coast with my pal Freddy Grosskreutz. Freddy was one of the best surfers from back there. He was also a member of the Hobie surf team and rode one of my models.

On that trip we stopped in New Jersey to see my old pal Tinker, of the pink house in Dana Point fame. He had moved there and owned Challenger Eastern surfboards.

Tinker was his same old more beatnik than hippie self and was raving about some kids that had a band and practiced in the back of his surfboard factory. He had built them amplifiers and a sound system and was managing them.

I was thinking, "yeah cool," and all that. But it turned out to be Bruce Springsteen, so I guess he was right. They were real good. I have always been a huge fan of Bruce Springsteen, the dude rocks.

Also, that year I met and did some work with the Beach Boys.

They hired Mickey Munoz and I to go up to Hollister Ranch with them to be in a promotional film they were making to push a new album that was getting released.

We went surfing and hung out and it was a pretty cool deal. On the way back we were riding with Bruce Johnston, Dennis Wilson, and Al Jardine and I think it was Bruce who said, "Hey you ought to come on tour with us, we will teach you how to sing."

I didn't take that very seriously and, as my total life was revolving around surfing at that time, I just laughed it off. In later life when things were more based around music I would have jumped at that chance. But not then. Mickey and I have mentioned that a few times, like "Well, we could have been Beach Boys...... but nooooo, hahaha." Oh well.

What did come out of that was a friendship with Dennis Wilson, the drummer.

* * *

Dennis was the only one who really surfed a whole lot and we sort of hit it off. He asked me to make him a board and so we put one together for him at Hobie's.

Right about the time it was finished, I was making a trip up to Hollister Ranch to go surfing and figured I would drop it off at his house on the way up. I called him in the morning and said I would be by later that day.

He lived in a big place off Sunset Boulevard right then and I showed up about 2 in the afternoon to drop the board. I was in a hurry to get going as I did not want to get stuck in the traffic leaving Los Angeles on the Ventura Freeway.

I knocked, and two naked girls opened the door. Nothing on at all.

They saw me with the board and cheerfully said, "oh you must be Corky, Dennis said you would be by. Come on in, he and Charley will be back in a few minutes. You wanna beer, smoke a joint, are you hungry?"

I had heard the rumor that Dennis had a bunch of girls living at his house, and they might have V.D.

I got a vibe that I should get going before I got into something that I shouldn't get into. So, I said thanks but no and I had to go, and thankfully I left.

Kind of a weird deal, but then in those days stuff like that would happen. Summer of love and all that.

There were actually girls that would hitchhike around just to give blow jobs to guys that would pick them up. Kinda like, "Hey, thanks for the ride. It's your lucky day." So I just kind of passed it off like just one of those things and didn't think all that much about it.

Years later when I was living in Sun Valley, Idaho, skiing and playing music, I had a period when I got sick and was in bed for a couple of weeks and had nothing to do but read.

I was reading the Helter Skelter book about Charles Mansion and all that stuff with the murders and when I got to the part in the middle where they had photos I freaked out.

"Holy shit, those chicks at Dennis Wilson's house were the Manson girls."

My skin crawled.

Manson and those girls had lived at Dennis's house for a while and indeed they all had a V.D. I was very happy and proud of myself for leaving that day.

The "Charley" that Dennis was out with was, obviously Manson. That whole "Helter Skelter" thing happened because Manson wanted to be a rock star.

Dennis tried to help him by getting him an audition with Terry Melcher, who was the son of Doris Day and the head of a record company.

When he got turned down, Manson got angry and decided that Melcher needed to be murdered and sent a group of his followers, including the chicks, over to his house to kill him.

What he didn't know was that Melcher had sublet his house out to Roman Polanski, who was off in Europe making a movie.

However his wife, the actress Sharon Tate, was there with some friends. That started the whole ugly nightmare. So anyway, there was that little deal that I narrowly avoided.

* * *

In the fall it became time to go back to Puerto Rico for the World titles. I was feeling really good about my chances too. I was in great shape and had very good equipment under me.

There was a little bit of a setback when they decided that the competition was going to be held at a spot that I had never got to surf when I was there before, as it was on a military base and was always closed to surfers. But they had gotten permission to use it for the contest.

There was a meeting between all the team managers to decide if they should hold it there or at "Maria's," which was the original site chosen. Maria's is a peak and offers both rights and lefts where Domes is strictly a right-hand wave.

Hevs McClelland had been sent down by our surfing association to be our manager and would speak for us. Hevs was a wonderful guy and an incredible contest announcer.

In this instance, he was very clueless as to the fact that our team was goofy-foot heavy and would stand a much better chance if the competition were held at Maria's. He was so clueless, in fact, that when the votes came down to a tie and it was his turn to vote he said, "I don't care, have it where George Downing says."

Now George was the manager of the Hawaiian team and it would obviously be better for them to have it at Domes and would give them a solid advantage over us. So, thanks to Hevs vote they decided on Domes.

Our guys were not happy about this and I think some let him know, I could have been one of those. Nonetheless, I was still feeling good about things.

I breezed through all my early rounds and into the semi-finals.

Then I made one critical mistake and it cost me my shot at the title. They were taking the scores from your best five waves for your total. I had three very good rides down and was on the fourth, also a good scoring wave. Towards the end of the ride as the wave was about to close out on some rocks I did what was called a "fly away kick out." This is where you get a lot of speed and actually launch your board out the top of the wave and it flies through the air.

This goes back to putting my board through the neighbor's kitchen window back when I was a kid in Surfside.

I am thinking I might get an extra point for height, and I probably did. But what I didn't see was that the wave behind the one I was on was already breaking and I launched my board so far that I could not swim to it before that next wave caught it and took it to shore.

In the time remaining in the heat, I could not get to it and get back out in time to catch a fifth wave.

Even with only four waves I barely missed advancing to the finals by only one or two points on all of the judges' cards, but that little error in judgment put an end to my hopes of winning that one.

I didn't make mistakes like that very often, but I sure did that day.

But all was not lost. I already had a great year and finished it off by winning the International Pro Championship in big surf at Steamers Lane in Santa Cruz for the second year in a row.

I was making good money and it was a good time in my life with my new family.

Corky in semi-final heat at the World Championship in Puerto Rico, 1968. Photo: LeRoy Grannis, courtesy of John Grannis.

CHAPTER 12

"Peaking" ~ 1969 – 1972

1969 was a year that I feel I probably did some of my best surfing on a day in and day out basis.

I was spending a lot of time with Rolf Aurness, who was the son of James Arness (dropped the u for some Hollywood kinda reason) who played Marshal Dylan on the hit T.V. series "Gunsmoke."

I had known Jim for a number of years from surfing at San Onofre and had watched Rolf grow into a solid world class surfer. Jim bought a home at Cotton's Point in San Clemente, and Rolf and I became regular surfing and skiing partners.

We traveled together up and down the coast and to Hawaii to surf. We also spent a lot of time at Mammoth Mountain skiing in the winter. He was a little younger than me, but we got along great and were able to push each other's surfing without blowing our friendship.

Rolf was a "goofy-foot," the same as me, but was one of those dudes who came along right about when there were some that could surf "backside," (back to the wave) actually better than they could facing the wave.

The great Australian surfer Wayne Lynch was like that and also coming into his own right about this same time. Rolf and Wayne were like the new hot young guns.

Surfing with Rolf was always a blast because we would try to outdo each other and be stoked with anything either of us did that was kinda good or better. We were competitive with each other but in a very healthy way, never any animosity or anything like that.

He always kicked my butt playing one on one basketball in his backyard, but I throttled him on my ping pong table.

That was also the year that President Richard Nixon purchased the Cotton's Estate, at Cotton's Point where I surfed all the time and turned it into the "Western White House."

When he was in town nobody could surf anywhere near there.

They had a big Coast Guard boat parked outside along with armed guards up and down the beach and helicopters flying overhead.

This threatened to cut into my surfing time at my favorite spot, so I hatched a plan.

I wrote a letter to the Secret Service explaining that I was the United States Surfing Champion and I trained at Cotton's Point, the surf spot directly in front of the new Western White House.

I asked for a pass to surf there, so I could train and represent the United States of America in worldwide surfing competitions.

To my amazement, they ran a background check on me and called me in for an interview. I cleaned up as best I could and went in and did the best version of a surfing patriot as I could. Voila! I got the pass.

This resulted in so many great days surfing there alone or with Rolf.

The home that his dad bought was in Cypress Shore, the private community that bordered the Cotton's Estate. Homeowners there were also allowed to surf.

At that time there was only Rolf, his dad, Grubby Clark who owed Clark Foam, a guy named Ralph Nichols, whose daughter I had dated for a while before I met Cheryl, and John Severson, who was the owner and publisher of SURFER Magazine.

John wasn't all that thrilled with the way things were going. Shortly after that he sold the magazine, his home at Cottons, and moved to Maui to spend the rest of his life painting and surfing.

Neither Grubby nor Ralph surfed much, as they were older and busy with, well, business, so the waves were pretty much mine and pretty much mine alone.

One afternoon when I had been having a nice session by myself, I ran into Richard Nixon on the beach.

He had been walking around wearing black shoes, black socks, royal blue shorts, white shirt, royal blue tie, and royal blue suit jacket.

He was flanked by a number of Secret Service agents. As I was coming out of the water, he spotted me and walked down and stuck out his hand.

"Sooooo, you are our surfing champion." He smiled and said graciously.

I smiled back, shook his hand and replied, "Soooo, you are our President."

We both laughed.

None of the Secret Service guys did, but I did see a couple of small grins. A little bit of small talk, and he told me to keep enjoying the surf, then we both went separate directions.

I couldn't help but think that it was cool to be buds with the pres. Yeah, I know things went bad later, but at that moment in time, I was pretty happy about the little meeting on the beach.

I had a solid year in competitions, winning the U.S. Men's Championship for the third time and U.S. Overall Championship for the 4th, along with the East Coast Championship and the first Smirnoff International Pro event in very big surf at Santa Cruz.

I also took third at the Makaha International in Hawaii that winter, which to me was probably one of my better accomplishments as a competitive surfer. It was not easy for a goofyfoot California boy to do well there, so, at least to me, this was really satisfying.

Corky winning U.S. Championship 1969.
Left to right: Gerry Lopez, Mike Purpus, Corky, Dru Harrison, Rolf Aurness.
Photo: LeRoy Grannis, courtesy John Grannis.

Corky with infamous surfing pioneer Jack O'Neill at Steamers Lane in Santa Cruz. Photo: LeRoy Grannis, courtesy John Grannis.

* * *

My pal Billy Hamilton had moved to the North Shore and was living in a house right in front of Pipeline during those years. He had met a great girl named Joanne and she was living with him, along with her son Laird. They called him Laird-John when he was young, the "John" part got dropped sometime later.

When I was staying on the north shore during the winters I sometimes got called into babysitting duty for Laird when Billy and Joanne wanted to go out and nobody better qualified was handy.

Babysitting Laird, who was really young but already ultra-high energy and super competitive, was an adventure. He really liked to play Checkers.

Playing a board game with Laird was sort of an art form.

If you beat him he would sulk off to his room and before long checkers would be pinging off the back of your head, followed by the checkerboard itself.

If you let him win he would know it and the same result would happen, only he wouldn't bother with sulking off to his room first.

So the challenge was to sort of make it as even as possible. Barely win one, then let him barely win one and sort of keep it really close with him coming out the eventual "grand champion."

I remember that his mom, Joanne liked to play "Jacks."

One day I was driving past their house when all of a sudden a whole bunch of jacks came flying out the upstairs window and hit the windshield of my car. I had to laugh. Obviously Joanne had just beaten Laird. I got outta harm's way before the little rubber ball or anything else rained down on me.

It wasn't unusual for Laird to toss a chair or even a couch, the kid was pretty gnarly.

When Billy and Joanne got married, Laird took Hamilton as his last name.

That kid grew into the greatest and most fearless big wave, no... GIANT wave, surfer of all time.

I have been in constant awe at the things he has done over the years and have proudly pointed to a few checkerboard scars on my head a number of times and stated, "Laird Hamilton?, yeah I know that dude."

* * *

My parents finally gave up fighting and split up right around then. It was sad, yet it was probably the best thing for both of them because they just never could get along at all.

My dad bought himself a place in a trailer park down by the beach just south of the pier in Huntington Beach and put a down payment on a nice little townhome for my mom up by the High School, also in Huntington Beach. I took over the payments for her as I was making pretty good money at that time.

Our house was still in my dad's name and I figured I would get around to getting it changed over into my name after I turned 21 and had time to do it. She was much happier on her own than she had been in years with my dad. And my dad, well he was now free to party to his heart's content without having to hear my mom scream at him for it. The one thing they would do though was both show up together to watch me surf each year at the United States Championship held there at the pier.

The one thing I always knew was that they were proud of me and were always there cheering me on.

* * *

In January 1970, right after coming back from Hawaii, I took off for Australia. They were going to hold the World Championships down there in May and I had never been there before, so I thought I would get down there early and get used to the place.

Upon arrival in Sidney, I took a taxi to a car lot and bought an old panel van that had been a meat delivery truck. It had a big cow painted on the side and had been geared very low so it could climb the hills with a heavy load of meat.

The good part of that thing was it was big enough to sleep inside and hold all my stuff and it ran very well and was reliable. The bad part was due to the low gearing the top speed was only about twenty- five miles an hour, a fact I didn't find out until I had already bought it and was on my way out of the downtown area and out to the north side. Oh well, I didn't really need to go fast anyway, I guess.

I headed out to a place called Whale Beach where there was a nice wedge-like left that came off a rock point and into a very pretty sandy cove.

My plan was to sleep in the van and then start finding my way around the next day. But, as luck would have it, I ran into a local surfer I had met in California named Chris "Bommy" Beachum, and he invited me to stay at his house in nearby North Avalon.

This turned out to be a very cool thing for me as Bommy knew everybody and where to go each day when we checked the surf.

I liked that area really a lot; it had great surf and really cool people.

My old pal Rodney Sumpter was living there too, with a family member of his who had a tennis court in his back yard. I spent some happy afternoons smacking the ball around with Rodney after surfing. Both Nat Young and Midget Farrelly lived nearby, but I really never saw them much while I was staying with Bommy.

After a couple of weeks, we got the idea to head up to Queensland to check out some of the great point breaks up there. In the cow-van this trip took 24 hours for what a normal car could do in about 10. Once we got there I knew I did not want to drive it back south when it became time to do so, I eventually traded it for an old Holden (Australian car) sedan with surf racks on it.

* * *

We arrived on the Gold Coast in a town called Burleigh Heads late one night and slept in the living room of a local surfboard builder named Dick Van Stralen.

In the morning I was woken by a girl who handed me a plate with a couple of pieces of toast with two big mushrooms on each of them. I said thanks and assumed that this was meant to be my breakfast.

But I was soon to learn that I had assumed wrong, very wrong.

A bunch of people came in a little bit later and saw the empty plate, asking, "What happened to the 'scrooms?'"

"Ah, they weren't for me?" I innocently replied.

They got kinda big-eyed and one guy said, "Wow mate, I never heard of anybody eating 4 of those big ones before!"

This is when I realized that these where "those" kind of mushrooms and maybe I might have just downed way more than I should have, which would have been NONE. Yikes.

But I was calmly assured by Bommy and the girl who had given them to me that everything would be okay, and I was just going to be in for an "interesting" day.

Now I have to admit I was a bit concerned. I smoked a little bit of pot, but was far from being your average stoner, or anything like that, and I was not very experienced in psychedelic adventures at all.

I really had no idea of what to expect but figured that whatever it was I could handle it one way or another. Again, I assumed wrong.

We loaded our boards onto somebody's car and headed out to surf a place called "Snapper Rocks." It was in the car on the ride to the beach that the "adventure" began.

As we were cruising along I was looking at the street, when all of a sudden it totally turned to multi-colored diamonds that started moving like that of a big long rattlesnake. I was thinking, "Wow, now I understand 'Lucy in the Sky with Diamonds.'"

Everything was more or less okay until we got to the beach and I got out of the car.

In the car I had known where I was, but outside the car I was totally lost in some crazy fantasyland, that I did not know at all.

The whole crew had grabbed their boards and paddled out, while I grabbed onto the hood of the car and held on for dear life.

After a little bit I realized that the car was black and it was really hot and I was getting fried like a piece of bacon.

This was not good.

So, I wandered down the beach and picked up a board. To this day I have no idea whose board it was.

So, I jumped in the water at the break in the rocks where it looked like people were paddling out from. A few strokes and I was in the surf zone and was immediately picked up by a broken wave that was reeling down the point.

Totally clueless, I tried to stand up and ran directly into an outcropping of rocks.

As I was lying there in the rocks after the wave subsided, all I could see where hundreds of crabs all grinning at me and snapping their pinchers.

Terrified, I jumped up and climbed over the rocks, dove onto a stretch of sand and curled into a fetal position, where I stayed for a couple of hours until Bommy and the other guys we were with came in and found me.

For the next three days and nights I had no idea where, or who I was, or what was going on in any way. I had sprained my wrist, and they had taken me to a hospital I was later told.

When it started to wear off and I realized who I was and what had happened I was positive that I had "fried my brain" and was destined to the nut house forever.

Thankfully it passed and I got back to normal, swearing to NEVER do that, or anything like it, again.

* * *

Bommy and I rented a little house on the side of the hill at Burleigh Heads and together we surfed all of the wonderful point breaks on the Gold Coast. Snapper Rocks was the most consistent and we spent most of our days there. That point pretty much ate my board though.

It was full of rocks and this was before we had surf leashes. I would surf until I lost my board and then spend all day repairing it so I could surf again in the evening until I lost my board and would spend half the night repairing it, so I could surf again in the morning.

This was a truly vicious cycle. Dick Van Stralen let me shape a board for myself in his surfboard factory that came out looking terrible. So we colored it purple and called it the "Mushroom Model." Dam thing worked really good though.

I realized that I really liked Australia and that I should be sharing this experience with Cheryl and our one-year-old son Clint.

We really didn't have the resources to pay for all of us to go, and that is why I went by myself. After being there for about a month I called Cheryl and told her I really wanted them to come down and for her to sell the Porsche to get the money.

I loved that car but loved them more and wanted them there to share this.

It turned out to be a truly, once in a lifetime experience.

With that Cheryl and Cint caught a flight into Brisbane. We hung out there and various places in Queensland. Where we a great time together as a family before heading back south to Sidney.

My pal Dru Harrison had just arrived and had hooked up with Bob MacTavishs ex-wife. We all went in on a killer house overlooking the beach between Whale Beach and Palm Beach.

It was up on a cliff and surrounded by water on three sides, amazing views. We hung out there and surfed all over Sidney for the next month and a half.

While there Cheryl got bit by a "funnel web" spider and her leg swelled up to the size of a pier piling, it was really scary.

One thing I did not like about Australia was all the snakes and spiders.

I swear that when you get off the plane they assign you 10,000 snakes and 10,000 spiders and most of them can kill you. If there are two things I don't like its snakes and spiders. They fall into the same category as giant squid and monster octopi.

Another thing that happened while we were there, was my son Clint riding his first wave on a surfboard.

It was a beautiful warm day at North Avalon. I put him on my board and floated him into a little swell where he rode laying down for about twenty or thirty feet. He got this giant smile and wanted to do it over and over, so we did.

A proud dad I was.

I'll never forget the stoke we both shared together that day.

***

When we got back to California that summer I made him a little board for his second birthday. It came out terrible, as I tried to shape it on the ground because it was too small for shaping racks. But he liked it and has it still to this day.

***

Finally, it was getting close to the time for the World Championships, which were to be held at Bells Beach in the southern state of Victoria. We all packed up and headed down to the little town of Torquay, which was the closest town to Bells Beach, and rented a "flat" (Aussie name for apartment) in a little two-story building.

Rolf Aurness had just arrived with his dad, and they rented the one next door to us. It was a lot colder down there than it had been in either Queensland or Sidney, and we had to start wearing full wetsuits and did a lot of shivering. But the surf in that part of the country is really good. We had a ton of great days leading up to the start of the big contest, which was in a way, when all hell broke loose. At least for me.

A couple of days before the contest was to start the rest of the American Team arrived in Torquay.

We all got together at a local pub for dinner and were having a great time until there was a sort of nasty confrontation with the lady who was serving us. It was over somebody asking for a little bit more butter for his role, and the lady rudely saying it would cost more if he wanted more butter, and it was actually really a lot more money for a little more butter.

When asked why it was so much, she, again very rudely, said, "you yanks are all rich, you can afford it."

This set off a number of rude and ruder remarks back and forth between her and us, and we wound up leaving.

I admit I said a couple of things I would have liked to take back.

I had been in that pub many times and had always had a good time and felt welcome. This was clearly a case of Anti-Americanism, and we all kinda reacted badly.

Turns out the lady was the wife of the owner, and he reported us to the local police.

I had been in there before, the only name she knew was mine, so they came over to our flat to talk to me about it. I did my best to explain, and they seemed happy with it but suggested that none of us go back to that pub while we were in town. I thought that was the end of it and everything was O.K. Wrong.

On the day before the contest started our team manager, guess who that was... yep, good ol' Hevs McClelland.

He had just got into town, and just so happened to stop into that very pub to have lunch. And guess who waited on him? Yep, the pub owner's wife.

When she heard his accent she said that the Americans had been in there a couple of nights before and were extremely rude to her and used bad language and had been kicked out.

Honestly, we were and did, but were not kicked out. We had left by our own choice and had paid our bill in full, probably not a good tip though.

When Hevs asked who it was, the only name she knew was mine, so she said, "It was Corky Carroll and THAT lot."

After what had happened in Puerto Rico two years before, relations between Hevs and myself had not been wonderful.

He held a big grudge about it and saw this as a perfect opportunity to get me for it, a fact that he would later admit to.

That evening was check-in for all the teams and there was going to be a big parade with all the teams in it.

When Hevs got to the hotel where all the officials and some of the teams were staying he got together with the contest committee and announced that he was kicking me off the US team for bad conduct.

When I got there to check-in I was taken into a small room and told that I was kicked out of the event and that I had 24 hours to leave town or I would be arrested.

Also, I was advised to leave the area immediately, or I would also be arrested. And that I would have no say in this. Nor could not lodge a protest, or even argue my case at all.

It was done and I had to leave right then and there. PERIOD. In total shock, I left.

In a short amount of time word got out about what had happened and most of our team, as well as some competitors from some of the other teams protested.

They refused to march in the parade. Most all were refusing to surf in the contest unless a meeting was called to investigate exactly what had happened and how to deal with it fairly.

So later that night a meeting was called, I was not allowed to attend. Cheryl went though, to find out exactly what would happen.

Turns out the couple who owned the pub found out about it too and showed up to beg them not to kick me out of the contest.

They said they had "rougher" chaps in their bar than me, and this stuff was just part of the business, and actually they liked me and this was not a fair shake. Too add, I wasn't the only one; it was pretty much everybody at the table who had been in on the altercation.

The wife did admit that she really did not mean to be so abrasive to us.

The International committee thought I should be reinstated. Finally ol' Hevs backed down. He did admit that he kind of had it in for me, and overreacted.

I was let back in and everybody went home happy. Cheryl told me the whole story and it was a huge relief. Big Time!

The bad part was that the local newspaper had a huge photo of me on the front page stating, "CARROLL OUSTED FROM SURF TITLES."

A smaller photo and caption at the bottom of the page was of Richard Nixon stating, "Nixon sends troops into Cambodia."

This naturally made its way back to California.

But that was not the end of it. On one of the first days of the contest, the local drug squad came to the beach and questioned our whole team about drug use and if we were all dealers.

They took us all into the back of an old ambulance and questioned each of us for like an hour, then later searched all of our rooms and cars, etc.

Of all the people that they could have found drugs on it turned out to be the one guy that never touched them at all. An excellent young surfer named Brad McCaul.

Turns out Brad was trying to score on some local chick, and she had left a small bag of pot in his room, or something close to this. In any case, he got busted but was let go with a slap on the wrist. I think they realized that he was not some druggie kingpin.

Problem was that this also hit the front page of the local newspaper.

A photographer was outside the ambulance they were questioning us in and just as I was getting out I saw him and put a towel over my head.

So, there is a huge photo of me with a towel over my head and the big headline, "DRUG SQUAD SWOOPS IN ON SURF TITLES."

Yes, this also made its way back to California. It wasn't all done yet.

A night or two later the owner of the hotel where most of the competitors and officials were staying got word that George Downing, again the manager of the Hawaiian team, had a young girl in his room.

So, this dude goes and opens George's door and storms in to bust him for having sex with an underage chick.

It's a total lie and George is by himself reading a book. The manager is totally miffed and confronts George.

Now, I should tell you right here, George is NOT a dude to mess with.

The guy says one too many things and George punches him and tosses him out of his room, breaking his arm in the process.

I love George Downing; he is one of the greatest surfers and people ever in surfing. And I love him because he, inadvertently, took some of the heat off of me.

The cops came and it turned out the hotel manager had no right to go into George's room uninvited and George had every right to toss the dude out. Case closed, but tensions were running high.

The contest itself went along fairly well and was moved from Bells Beach to a beach break about two hours away called Johanna for the last day.

I had made it to the semifinals and had a very close decision.

It came down to my best ride, a pretty good backside tube ride that I thought won the heat for me.

The Hawaiian and California judge gave me a perfect 20 (out of 20) on it. The Australian and Peruvian judges gave me a 4 and the remaining judge, I don't remember who that was, gave me a 12.

I wound up missing the final by a point or two and finished in a tie for seventh place.

Was this blatant mis-scoring a result of all of the previous chaos that week?

Maybe, probably, but it was what it was.

Thankfully my pal Rolf Aurness had a great day and won the contest over local favorites Midget Farrelly, Nat Young and Peter Drouyn.

We left Australia right after the contest was over, even though we had planned on staying another month to see more of the country.

I was burnt out and just wanted to get home and get back to our normal life. I did love Australia, but the whole scene with the World Contest was more of a nightmare than fun.

But more nightmares were waiting for me at home. Turns out Hevs had been in touch with his wife Marge.

Marge was a great women's surfer and the mother of Candy and Robin Calhoun, who were also great surfers in their own rights.

Hevs had not been, shall I say, completely honest in his assessment of what had happened.

Sadly, ol' Hevs had made me out to be a really bad representative of the country and surfing in general.

Marge was, on the other hand, was a great friend with Jim Gilloon, who was the manager of Hobie Surfboards and my immediate boss.

Hobie himself was pretty much out of the surfboard part of the business by then and doing his Hobie Cat Company thing, which was going big time. Marge telling Jim all this and him seeing the newspapers totally outraged him.

Jim would also later tell me that it always pissed him off when I would roar into the factory in my Porsche with my hair wet and pick up a royalty check that was way more than what he was making and then roar back out to go surfing. I never realized that and thought we had always been close pals.

He kind of had a chip on his shoulder towards me about that and all this stuff he heard from Marge about me in Australia, and the newspaper clippings totally put him over the top.

A couple of days after I got home and was getting ready for the upcoming contest season, he called me in and read me the riot act.

I had shamed Hobie, as he saw it.

I think he really wanted to fire me but, as my models were still their bestseller and I was making the company a lot of money he really couldn't.

What he did do was tell me they would be cutting back on advertising my boards and using me in the ads for the foreseeable future.

"Until all this blows over," were his words.

Now in my mind, there really wasn't an "all this."

It had been totally blown out of proportion by Hevs and Marge.

In the overall picture, the only thing that really happened was that I had not won the contest. But Jim was convinced that I had been a really bad person and wanted to cut me back as far as Hobie surfboards was concerned.

Hobie really had no clue as to most of this, as I would find out in later years.

Hobie was always great to me and treated me fairly. I have always had nothing but the greatest respect for him.

* * *

The offshoot of this was that after a few months I decided that it would be better if I had my own brand.

Jim was fine with that, and it was agreed that we would launch *"CORKY CARROLL SPACESTICKS"* and Hobie would build and sell them. No full-page ads, just little ones in the back of SURFER Magazine.

We did hit it good with the "twin fin" model, and I was able to still make a living and it all worked pretty well.

* * *

I had a decent contest season, taking second place in the U.S. Championship behind Brad McCaul and again winning the Overall U.S. title for the 5th year in a row.

I also placed in the finals at Makaha in Hawaii again so, although it had not been the best of years, it was an okay one.

* * *

During the winter of 70/71, I found myself both skiing and playing music a lot more.

I had always loved to ski and was spending way more time on the slopes than I had done in recent years. My interest in music was really coming to the forefront.

I hung out at the local music clubs and was very actively trying to become a decent guitar player.

My main focus was still surfing, that was not in question. Playing music was rapidly becoming an obsession that I could not say no to.

It had always been there but had been pushed back until about then. No longer. I sort of made the decision that after my surfing career ran its course I wanted to get into music. I was really serious about it.

Then a funny thing happened that I have, regretted to this day.

A good friend of mine named Steve Walden had become partners with this rich dude who had made a fortune in batteries. His name was Dick Lippincott.

Evidently this dude was putting a lot of money into Steve's surfboard business in Huntington Beach. He had purchased the old Plastic Fantastic board factory and his goal was to rock the surfboard industry.

His thought was that he was really smart and everybody in surfing was not.

Steve recruited me to bring CC Spacesticks over to his new company that was going to be called DYNO surfboards. They would produce Walden and CC Spacesticks. They also went after David Nuuhiwa.

I met with Dick Lippincott and his plan sounded pretty good as he laid it out.

He offered me about double what I was making with Hobie at the time and said he would put a ton of money into advertising my boards.

Sounded too good to pass up, so I went for it.

Over the course of a few weeks, I recruited a number of top surfboard craftsmen to come over to Dyno and build the boards.

It was all looking like it was gonna work out fine, until I went in to get my first paycheck.

Have you ever heard the term, "get it in writing?"

My check was 20% of what Lippincott had offered me.

I asked him what the deal was, and he seemed shocked. He said that what he offered me was "what I might make."

This is when I learned that this guy could look you square in the eye and tell you the biggest lie you ever heard, knowing that you know it's a lie, and expect you to believe it because he was saying it.

He made himself out to be a Christian and read the bible and all that, but this dude turned out to be one of the biggest BSers I have ever come in contact with.

But what was done, was done and I was stuck. What a blunder.

*　*　*

It was the summer of 1971 and the beginning of the last chapter in my competitive professional surfing career.

Poor Steve had also been duped by this man as well as David Nuuhiwa, who had also come on board at the same time.

I was having a solid year competitively speaking and winning most of the surf contests in California.

As fortune would have it, about then, Jack Haley had hired me to play music in at his restaurant, Captain Jacks.

This was my first paying gig, and I was all over it.

I also hooked up with a pal of mine from Newport Beach that was a great blues harmonica player and singer named Al Oakie. We played during intermission at some of the surfing movies showing in the area.

* * *

Things were picking up music-wise and the more I got into it, the more I got INTO it. My main drawback was I really could not sing worth a dam back then.

I can proudly say that all these years later I have gotten to be a very good singer and feel great doing it.

In those early years I could play guitar okay, but my singing sucked.

Nonetheless, a little thing like that did not stop me at all. I was totally going for it.

I was hooked and convinced that I could eventually be good.

* * *

After a successful competitive surfing season in California. I took the family to the North Shore to spend a few months that winter.

My actual day-to-day surfing was still very good, and I was really feeling good in Hawaii that winter.

I wound up placing at Makaha again plus made the finals of the Duke Kahanamoku Invitational and took 3rd place in the first Pipeline Masters event. Probably my best season on the North Shore.

Now I should probably tell the story, behind the story, of a little side event to one of the Pipeline Masters.

The final heat was made up of myself, Gerry Lopez, Billy Hamilton, Jeff Hackman, Jock Sutherland and Jimmy Blears.

The surf had not been very good during the beginning of the waiting period to hold the event.

One morning I pulled up at the park by Pipeline to check it out.

Gerry Lopez was there too, and we both were commenting that the surf was not nearly good enough to hold the event. He asked me if I thought they would hold it anyway.

I said I didn't think so; the wind and swell were both wrong. He agreed and we both left.

A couple of hours later they came and got me at Mark Martinson's house, where I was staying.

Evidently Freddy Hemmings, who was the contest director, had info that the surf was only going to get worse as the time period went on and that he was going to run the event that day.

As it turned out he was correct, the following days were even worse than this day, which was not very good at all.

Everybody showed up except for Gerry Lopez, and nobody was able to reach him.

Remember we did not have cell phones back then. He had gone back to town and was not near a phone.

Fred asked me whom we could get to replace him.

A good surfer from Laguna Beach named Mike Armstrong just happened to be in the water and happened to get a really good ride at that exact moment.

I looked at Fred and said, "how about him?" So they got Mike to take Gerry's spot.

They held the contest in the wrong direction, wrong wind, small Pipeline. Mike took second place behind Jeff Hackman and ahead of me.

All in all, it was just one of those things that happened, the top three would be invited back the next year so it was a victory of sorts.

Somehow, someway, a story developed that I had "tricked" Gerry into leaving the area on the contest day. Like I had told him the contest would not be run when I knew it really was.

I have no idea how this story got started, but it did, and it sort became a legend of the first Pipeline Masters. When I first heard it I was furious, it was so NOT true and wrong.

In later years I embraced it as kind of funny.

It was like if Magic Johnson and Michael Jordon show up outside the stadium during the NBA finals and Magic told Jordan the game was called off that day and Jordon believed him and left and missed the game.

At the time this happened I would never have done that. In my huge surfing ego brain, I believed I could win it and wanted to beat those guys, especially Gerry who was the favorite, at that spot.

When I was much older the thought of pulling something like that off seemed much cooler, so I became not so upset about the story. But the truth was that it was not true.

Thankfully Gerry came out with a story in one of the magazines backing me up and saying it was not true and what had really happened was exactly as I said it was. But it was a fun story while it lasted.

* * *

After another good year on the contest circuit in California, I went back to the North Shore with high hopes to do well over there again. I was feeling confident in big surf and was in very good condition physically.

Unfortunately, after a being over there for only a few days I stepped on a broken bottle getting out of the car to go surfing one afternoon. I was with Mike Doyle, Nat Young and another great Aussie surfer named Keith Paul.

It cut the bottom of my heel really badly, and I was bleeding big time. Mike and Nat looked at it and shrugged it off and went surfing. Keith saw it was bad and drove me to the hospital.

It was worse than I thought, and I got 17 stitches and was told to not go in the water for at least a month and to keep it super clean because everything gets infected over there with the heat and humidity. So, I went home and didn't get to surf in any of the contests in Hawaii that winter.

* * *

At the beginning of 1972, I had no idea this would be my last year surfing competitively. I was still winning most of the contests and was at the top of the rankings in California. I had started that year winning an event in Oxnard and was feeling as good or better than ever as far as my surfing went.

The deal with Dyno was not a great thing, the dude never did give me a raise so the whole "what I could make" thing was a sham. I spent most of the time trying to avoid contact with him. They were making plenty of boards, and I was getting ripped off, as well as Steve Walden and David. But it was what it was, and I was just living with it, as I had nothing better to fall back on.

* * *

Sometime during that winter, I got an offer from a guy in Australia to put up the money for me to put together a group of surfers who played music and to do an album. So, I got Dennis Dragon involved to record it.

Dennis was the son of conductor Carmen Dragon and also the younger brother of Daryl Dragon who was the original keyboard player for the Beach Boys and became Captain in Captain and Tennille. He was an expert recording engineer and had the equipment to travel up and down the coast to record the different players on the album.

Dennis would later become the brainchild and drummer for the SURF PUNKS who were signed by none other than Motown Records.

We started our own record label and called it "Rural Records." Our logo was a telephone pole with a pigeon sitting on it.

Later on, Jackson Browne made a funny comment stating that it was interesting that we had a pigeon on the pole when we were based in Capistrano. San Juan Capistrano is famous for being the place the "swallows" come back to every year.

I love Jackson Browne and am a huge fan of all of his music. I had known him in our younger years surfing in Seal Beach, but I had kind of forgotten him.

When his song "Doctor my Eyes" came out, and he was starting to get known he did a concert at my local folk club in San Clemente, the Four Muses, and I went to see him. But I didn't know he was the same kid I had surfed with years before.

I was standing at the refreshment counter getting something, and he walked up and started talking to me like we were old pals. I knew that I knew him, but I could not think of who in the heck he was. Just somebody I had known years before and I could not think of his name. Looking for clues I asked him what he was up to these days. He said he was playing music. I said that was cool and asked if he was playing anywhere. He said he was playing THERE that night. I say, "Wow, are you playing with Jackson Browne?" He laughed and said, "Uh yeah, I am Jackson Browne." Oops, kind of embarrassing moment. But all was good and the next day I took him surfing with me at Cotton's, and we rekindled the old friendship. I also met David Lindley for the first time, another musician I am a big fan of and become a little closer friend with, in later years. I will get to all that later.

The album came out and was called CORKY CARROLL AND FRIENDS. It featured Raymond Patterson playing slack key style guitar and uke, Al Oakie doing blues, Herbie Torrens, Dave Rullo and Jon Close, who had a cool little band in San Diego, some chick who Dennis had something going with that lived by Malibu, and played open stringed guitar and had nice boobs, and me doing some instrumental guitar pieces that I made up.

For some reason, they like this album in Japan and it has come out over the years a few times on different Japanese labels. I have done a lot better stuff over the years but in Japan, they keep wanting that one.

I spent a lot of time hanging out and playing music at the Four Muses and met tons of cool people and other musicians.

It was run by Jim and Mary Jenkins, who were two of the greatest people I had ever known.

Mary was a wonderful folksinger and was the person who first taught me how to "finger pick."

I spent years just banging away strumming chords, but in the end, I would totally switch over to a total fingerstyle method of playing guitar. That was still decades down the line. Nonetheless, it was Mary who set me on that path in the first place.

They held open microphone nights at the Four Muses that they called "Hoots." I became the M.C. for the Hoot nights. We had a lot of really good musicians come to play on those nights.

One night a local band that was just getting started from Laguna Beach showed up and blew the house away. They were called "Honk," and my childhood jamming pal Tris Imboden was the drummer. This would become one of my favorite bands of all time, along with the Rolling Stones.

* * *

Another thing that happened for me musically that year was my singing debut on National Television.

I was on the Merv Griffin Show one night with a bunch of other athletes from different sports. As I am sort of accustomed to doing, I made some jokes and generally hammed it up as much as I could. Merv got a lot of mail about me, saying, "this kid is funny, you should have him back on."

One of the things he had asked me on that first show was what I did when I wasn't surfing. I told him I was a musician and played at Captain Jacks down in Sunset Beach. I think he thought I meant on Sunset Blvd or something, I don't know. But a couple of months later he called me up one afternoon and asked if I could come on the show that night and do a song. Somebody had canceled at the last minute, and he had a spot to fill.

So, I grabbed my guitar, jumped in the car and beat it through traffic an hour to get to CBS TV in time for the taping of the show.

When I walked in I noticed that his band was a lot bigger than the last time I had been on. It turns out that he was doing a theme show on singers who have sold over a million records, and I am coming on, in contrast, as a guy making his television singing debut. Holy poopoo.

Did I mention that my singing sucked in those days? I wanted to run and actually tried to sneak out the bathroom window, but it was on the second floor, so I was stuck.

But on the wall in one of the stalls, there were some funny limericks written down. A little off color but not so bad that you couldn't say them on television. As this well-known soul singer was on just before me doing almost the exact same blues song I was gonna do, only a kazillion times better.

I instantly made up a really short song, 57 seconds, using the limericks off the wall. I asked Merv to let me talk before I sang; normally it's the other way around. He asked me why and I just said trust me, and he did.

So, I told some jokes and got the crowd laughing and sort of explained my predicament. Then I got on the piano and did a standard twelve-bar blues, singing the words to the funny limericks. The band, which turned out to be all the *PLAYBOY Magazine* Jazz Poll winners jumped right in and backed me.

It was short, dumb, funny and I finished it up with a Jerry Lee Lewis thumb roll, tripped over the piano stool and crawled back into my chair. Everybody was laughing hard enough to not really be concerned that I totally sucked.

Merv was very happy and said I could be on his show anytime I wanted and do anything I wanted. I would be a fill-in guest another time or two while he was still on the air. My friends who saw the show said I should never sing again, but I was funny and should stick to jokes. This was kind of the theme of my early years in music.

I think in order to succeed in stuff like this you have to be willing to embarrass yourself in front of zillions of people and not be afraid to do it. Sometimes you get away with it and sometimes ya don't, but you have to keep coming back, nonetheless. At least until either you get good at it or realize that you never will and give up. For some, it takes longer to reach that crossroads than others.

* * *

They held the World Championship in San Diego again that year. I was the top-rated California surfer and was one of the favorites to win it as I was surfing well and had a lot of momentum from another solid competition season.

It was a very strange contest from the time it started. There was a huge south swell running from a big storm off of Baja.

Unfortunately, the angle of the swell was so south that it was missing San Diego entirely. At Newport Beach, farther up the coast in Orange County, the waves were 15 feet.

However, down in San Diego, it was flat. At the far north end of San Diego County, in a town called Oceanside, the swell was hitting at least a little bit.

There were surfable waves there and, as it was still in San Diego County, they decided to move the competition up there. It was a good move and the contest was going along well until they got to the last day.

For the final rounds, they decided they had to move back into the city of San Diego so the crowds could be there, television and all of that. The fact that there was no surf did not matter at all, it was the show that was more important. Being more than less unhappy that the World Championship, the event that was supposed to be the top event on earth, was going to be decided in waves less than one foot and that the organizers didn't care one bit about it as long as it went off smoothly was really sad.

In my semifinal heat, I paddled out and sat in the spot where a tiny wave broke every now and then and waited for one to come.

When there were about five minutes left in the heat, the other guys paddled right next to the beach and were trying to ride these tiny little beach lappers, just to get some sort of score.

I just sat there and pondered that if this was what "PROFESSIONAL" surfing had come to then maybe it was time for me to hang up my jersey and call it a career.

The horn sounded to end the heat, and with it my competitive surfing life.

The ride was over.

* * *

A couple of weeks later Dyno Dick called me into his office to tell me he was cutting back and could no longer pay me my 20% of what I was supposed to get salary wise, but if I wanted to stay on he would give me a couple of bucks a board for the ones with my name on them.

This was just a further way to try and rip me off, he being the business genius that he thought he was and being smart while all surfers were not. I didn't go for it and ended the Dyno relationship for good. He was not happy when I filed for unemployment and he had to pay.

CHAPTER 13

"The Mountains" ~ 1973 - 1975

So, what to do now?

Here I was an unemployed retired pro surfer.

The unemployment money was not that bad and also Cheryl was working at a local Mexican food restaurant making pretty good tips. I started giving surfing lessons on Saturdays at a local beach and was making a little bit playing music. I had put together a little acoustic band that included a very talented young female singer named April Fuladosa, a flute player from Australia named Lindsey Farr, an amazing violin player named Doug Kratz and a bassist named Glenn Candy. The popular San Diego D.J., Gabriel Wisdom, came onboard as our manager. We did a couple of concerts, one of which was opening for Dan Hicks and his Hot Licks on a night when he didn't show up. Lucky we got on, off and outta there before the huge crowd found out he wasn't gonna show.

Aside from the band, April and I had a few gigs playing in restaurant bars in Orange County and San Diego. Along the way I became friends with another amazing violin player from Laguna Beach named Doug Miller, who would become a lifetime friend and a very important member of my musical family.

Between everything, we really didn't make much money but somehow we got through the winter.

Corky was featured in the SAN DIEGO READER just before one of his first concerts at the University of San Diego. This was at the time he teamed up with popular San Diego D.J. Gabriel Wisdom as his musical manager.

* * *

One morning during the end of May I was out surfing on a good, but really crowded, day at my favorite spot, Cotton's Point. Guys had been dropping in on me over and over and it was hard to have much of a good time with so much congestion.

A nice set wave came along, and I had been waiting a long time for it, so I caught it and dropped to the bottom of the wave setting up for the turn and climb into the pocket.

Some guy took off on the other side of the peak where he had no chance of making it, I was thinking he was going the opposite way as that would have been the correct thing to do. But this dude went down the wave the wrong way and kicked his board as hard as he could right at me. It hit me in the back of my leg and knocked me off.

When I came up the guy was screaming at me and calling me names. Turns out this guy had just moved from Florida and thought he was some hot shit or something. I just got out of the water at that point and went home.

On the way, I plotted out the future.

* * *

I had always loved to ski and never had the chance to spend a full winter in the mountains, this was the time to do it.

My plan was to drive to Sun Valley, Idaho, Steamboat Springs and Aspen, Colorado. I would then pick which place I wanted to be at and get myself some sort of job and a place to live.

At that point, I would bring Cheryl and Clint up, and we would spend a year in the mountains. The beginning of summer was the ideal time to get a job and a place to live in a ski resort town.

So, I loaded up my van and the next morning I took off on the drive to Sun Valley, my first stop on the "pick a place to live tour." My old friend Dick Barrymore, the same dude who had built my first two surfboards, was living there and had offered me a place to stay for a few days.

Dick had become one of the leading ski filmmakers, along with Warren Miller. I got there the day Dick and his wife Betsy were hosting a big party because they needed a shed moved from one side of their house to the other. The party was an excuse to get a whole bunch of people over there to help lift and move the shed. The Barrymore's were Sun Valley high society and all kinds of town biggies were there.

By the end of the party, I had a job working in the Scott Ski Boot factory, and a cool apartment very close to the ski lifts in the Warm Springs area of town.

I also had an application in for the new Chart House restaurant that had just opened. No need to go any further, I was all set up right there in Sun Valley. I called Cheryl and told her to put the house up for rent and as soon as she had a tenant to load up her car, a very cool early 50s Plymouth sedan that we scored cheap and had nicknamed the "Zub", and for her and Clint to come on up.

I settled into the apartment and began working the rivet machine on the assembly line at Scott Ski Boots. It was a 10 hour a day, 4 days a week job. On two of my days off, I worked for Betsy Barrymore's brother doing construction. Actually, I didn't do any constructing myself; I was strictly a lumber carrier. This was fine and dandy until one day I was carrying a bunch of two by fours across a beam in the upstairs of a house we were working on. The beam twisted and I fell right through the kitchen ceiling. A few cuts and bruised ribs and that was the end of that job, thankfully.

But the lucky part was right at that same time a job opened up washing dishes at the new Chart House. This was way better as I could work at Scott boots in the daytime and then head over to the Chart House at night. It wasn't very glamorous, but I was just stoked to be there and getting a foot in the door.

One night I was in the kitchen neck-deep in dirty dishes, probably had lettuce in my hair or something equally greasy, scrubbing away as hard as I could. Dick Barrymore comes in along with none other than Hevs McClelland and his wife Marge. They all take one look at me and started cracking up. Dick, who was a world-class funny dude, bellows out, "And this, ladies and gentlemen, is the world-famous dishwasher CORKY CARROLL!!!!" I threw a half a baked potato at him and they walked out in hysteria.

Later Hevs and I had a long talk and made up.

* * *

This was sort of the beginning of the long and very difficult job of losing my enormous surfing ego, something that I had worn bravely, or maybe abrasively is the better word, since winning that first surf contest at San Clemente when I was 14. But then, I never claimed to NOT be obnoxious. I just claimed that it was in the spirit of funniness and expected that people would know the joke, even if they didn't. And if they didn't get it then it was THEIR problem and not mine, I was the cool one.

This was such a difficult attitude to get over and it would take many, many years for me to come to grips with it.

But that night in my little dish washing bay at the Chart House in Sun Valley when Barrymore, Hevs and Marge were so happy to see me humbled and I had to laugh at myself along with them, instead of taking offense, it was probably a start to deflating my Jupiter sized head.

As I started to work my way up from dishwasher to busboy I let the job at the ski boot factory go, as they were overlapping too much and my bosses at both places didn't like it if I left early or was late coming in. Also, one of the cocktail waitresses, who also sang and played guitar, and I put together a little duo and played in the bar on Saturday nights.

So that summer, while I had a lot of time on my hands in the daytime, I started playing a lot of tennis at the local tennis club in Warm Springs and took some lessons. I really liked it and played every day. It was sort of the beginning to about a twenty-five year obsession with that sport, only I wasn't totally aware of it yet.

It took Cheryl a couple of months to get the house rented out and get her and Clint packed up. But in August they showed up, and we started setting ourselves up for the coming winter.

By November, I had worked my way up to be a waiter at the Chart House, the perfect job for a dude wanting to ski all day, and Cheryl had got hired as a hostess.

I also got a fantastic gig playing music for one hour a week at a welcoming party that the Ski School threw every Monday evening from 5 to 6 o'clock. I got paid ten dollars, free dinner and best of all, a free season ski pass. How great was that?

By the time ski season started we had Clint enrolled in a preschool that took the kids skiing in the afternoons, and we had the perfect jobs working at night at the Chart House so the days were free to ski. This was really working out better than I could have imagined. I skied 120 of the 122 days the mountain was open that winter.

The following summer we lucked out and scored a really cool house to rent in the same area. It had four bedrooms and was on a natural hot spring. One of the bedrooms was separate from the rest of the house and had its own entrance. We had really cheap rent and all the utilities were included, plus we were able to rent out the separate bedroom for more than half of the rent. This made things way better as far as making ends meet, and we decided that we would stay in Sun Valley for longer than we had planned. The people renting our house at the beach were fine with staying, so it just worked out perfectly to prolong our mountain adventure.

More tennis that summer and I also discovered it was only a ten- hour drive to the great left-hand point where I had liked to surf in Oregon. There were a few other surfers turned skiers working at the Chart House with me, and we did a number of "get off work at 11, drive all night to Oregon, surf a couple of days and get back to work" surf pilgrimages.

This, along with finding out I could actually surf a wave in the river behind our house, kept my surfing hunger satisfied. At least until I lost my board one day in the river and it took off and I never found it.

With the tennis, skiing and working on music, I was pretty happy with just getting a few weeks in the spring and fall, when everything was closed, to go back to the beach and ride as many waves as I could. Surfing was not at the forefront of my attention right then.

That summer I got into the management program at the Chart House.

Under the guidance of a very cool dude named John Alderson, who was our manager, I learned how to do everything from making the secret thousand-island salad dressing to being able to semi accurately estimate the amount of salt in all the saltshakers on the tables during monthly inventory. It also involved cooking, tending bar, making schedules and a whole lot of other stuff that really took a lot of time and effort.

It was a great education, but by the time ski season came around I realized that I wasn't as dedicated, or as good, at this as I should have been and that this was not the way I wanted to spend the winter. I wanted to ski every day and play music. So, I went back to waiting tables and was, once again, a very happy camper.

Clint was in kindergarten at Wood River Elementary School, which is a very cool school. Every afternoon the teachers took the classes up on the mountain to ski. It was classic to see. The teacher would be leading a single line of a bunch of little kids all doing the same turns and taking the same path that the teacher set up.

In the spring they held a big race called the "Kinder-Cup." It was amazing how good these little kids could ski by that time, including Clint. This was really a pretty cool life we were having up there, not a way to get ahead or make some sort of financial future or anything like that though. It was definitely a "for the moment, and for the lifestyle" kinda thing, the kinda thing that sort of would become my mantra for life as time went on.

My old surf pal Mike Doyle moved up there that winter. He got a little house in Haley, which was the next town south of Ketchum (the actual town that Sun Valley is in.)

Mike had spent the past few years developing a "mono" ski. This was one big wide ski that you placed the bindings side by side on, like gluing two skis together or something like that.

In soft snow those things were incredible, and Mike had become insanely good on it. He had two of them and loaned me one of them.

You could go way faster on the mono-ski than you could on two skis in "powder" snow, there was no doubt about it. Doyle was so fast and so good that pretty much nobody could stay up with him unless they were also on one. One day I was doing my best to follow him down one of the bowls and blew up and dislocated my shoulder. That kept me down for a while and cut my skiing days to only about 80 that year.

Joey Cabell came up and skied with Mike for a little while and those guys were just blowing everybody away when there was powder.

Barrymore took Mike, Joey, Roger Yates from Newport Beach, and me over to Jackson Hole to film us all on the mono-skis. It was a great session except I was still in so much pain from the shoulder injury that I had a hard time. I did manage to get in one shot in the movie though and also did a little music for the soundtrack. It was called *"The High Cost of a Free Ride."*

That title seemed to tattoo itself into the backside of my brain, more of that lifestyle mantra.

Doug Miller, the violinist from Laguna Beach that I had become friends with back at the beach, showed up one day and spent a few weeks with us taking photos and hanging out.

Doug is not only a great violinist but also a world class photographer and artist. He is a bit wacky, to say the least, doesn't drive or anything like that. But he is a total genius at the stuff he does do.

We loved him and really enjoyed his visit that winter. During that stay, we played a little bit of music together and it was very cool.

Right then I didn't really know what a large part Doug would have in the early years of my actual musical career.

In the spring when the ski lifts closed down, as did most of the town, for what they called "Spring Slack," the guy who owned the house we were renting came to me and told me he decided he wanted to sell it and offered me first chance at it.

It was a very reasonable offer, but it kind of took me by surprise and also made me realize that we had a big decision to make if we were going to think about this at all.

Did we want to live in the mountains from then on?

In order to buy that house, we would have to sell the one in Capistrano Beach and that would mean bailing out on the beach entirely. He gave us a month to think it over. We headed back to California to spend "slack" and give all this serious thought.

It was the beginning of May. As luck would have it a really good south swell hit right then and I scored ten days in a row of perfect ten-foot surf at Cotton's Point.

This had a big impact on my decision as it made me realize that no matter what I did, be it ski, play tennis, play music, whatever; I was a surfer first and foremost. That is what I am. Top of the head to bottom of the feet, in the heart, mind, and soul for as long as I live.

The choice was clear, and Cheryl agreed, time to move home.

CHAPTER 14

"Finding the Beat"

It was early summer 1975. We settled back into our home in Capistrano Beach and set about figuring out what we were going to do to survive. I got a job as a waiter at a new restaurant in San Clemente called the City Yard Bar and Grill and another teaching guitar and piano at a local music store. Cheryl got hired as a waitress at Henry's Mexican food on Pacific Coast Highway in Capistrano Beach. Her parents lived on the hill right above our house and were great at babysitting Clint when we were working.

I knew it was time for me to try to do something more meaningful with my music than just playing in restaurants and bars and decided to try to put together a band. I got together with Doug Miller and with his help and that of Jim Jenkins, who owned the Four Muses Club, we organized "Corky Carroll and the Funk Dog Surf Band."

I had loved the set up that Dan Hicks had with "Dan Hicks and his Hot Licks," which was a sort of jazz/swing band. He had two hot girl backup singers called the "Lickettes," and a killer violin player named Sid Page. My idea was to have that same sort of lineup but do more surf rock kinda music. We got three girls to be the "Corkettes," one of which was Cheryl. Doug would play "lead" violin. We were unique in the fact that we had no lead guitar player; I was strictly rhythm in those days.

I wrote a bunch of really corny surf/beach songs, and we constructed a show that has as much musical comedy as anything else. We got a fantastic young drummer named Matt Magiera and an excellent Piano Player named Stuart Rabinowitz. Doug was living in a house owned by Stuart's mom and Stu had been playing up in the San Francisco area doing jazz. He came down and listened to what we were trying to do and thought we might have a shot at doing something, so he came aboard.

We put an ad in the paper and were lucky to score a really fine bass player, also a very cool dude, named Jack Finn. The original Corkettes were Cheryl, Debbie Green, and Desi Bush. Cheryl and Debbie remained through all of the transformations of the band. After Desi there was a fiery redhead named Becky Gaulden and finally a very well trained and a pretty chick singer named Kathy Brown. When we had that last set of Corkettes, Cheryl went by Loretta Lavender, to go along with Debbie Green and Kathy Brown.

The band all wore matching Hawaiian shirts that we had got from Dave Rochlen at Jams, and I had a red blazer with palm trees done in sequins on the lapels and a big "Aloha" on the back. The Corkettes wore these killer Carmen Miranda type of outfits that they made themselves. They worked out some great dance routines to each of the songs, some of which were surfing moves, and had amazing three part harmonies. The whole thing was a real show.

With this line up we played all over Southern California at High Schools, Colleges and small clubs which included the Golden Bear in Huntington Beach, the Bluebird Café in Santa Barbara, the Back Door in San Diego, the Four Muses, The Basement in Orange and the Ice House in Pasadena. At the Ice House we had a regular revolving one night every four weeks deal that included the "Ramones" and two other bands.

Corky performing with the Funk Dog Surf Band at the Four Muses Club in San Clemente, Ca. Photo: Doug Miller.

Headlining at the GOLDEN BEAR in Huntington Beach. The "Bear" was one of Southern California's most popular Music Venues in the 1960's and 1970's. Photo: Doug Miller

We also did the *"Gong Show"* two times. The first time we won and got invited back a few months later. That time we got gonged by a dude named Rex Reed about 15 seconds into the really silly surf song we were about to do. I don't think I even got a word out of my mouth when he hit the gong. We really had not had a chance to be either good or bad at that point, but he thought we were going to be one of the "gag" acts that Chuck Barris used to stick into those shows and wanted to nail it before it started. It was really embarrassing and for years I had to deal with people, mostly my friends, loving to bring it up.

"Hey man, I heard ya got gonged on the gong show, hahahaha." I think many of these were the same friends that when I first started singing used to suggest that I didn't. But I guess if your pals can't give you a bad time who can? It's that, "you can't be afraid to embarrass yourself in front of thousands of people," thing that I had learned was part of my inner persona. I did it many times and just kept coming back for more.

We did a mini-tour on the East Coast that was both a ton of fun and a nightmare for me at the same time. I had a really bad cold and sore throat. Getting there and getting back with the whole band and equipment was really hard to organize and actually pull off. We played concerts at the Venus Theater in Ocean City, Maryland and the Virginia Beach Convention Center in Virginia Beach before heading down to play a few nights in a very cool beach bar in Nags Head, North Carolina.

On this trip we hooked up with a great singer and guitar player named Poul Pederson, who I had met and played with a little bit back at the Four Muses Club. He was in Ocean City when we played there, and we invited him to sit in with us. He fit in really well and decided to join the band. It was a really fun trip in all aspects other than I was sick and could hardly sing at all.

The guys who put the tour together, Jay Evilsizor and a dude who went by simply Uncle Bob were really fun and cool dudes to hang out with. They became longtime pals of mine after that.

Corky Carroll - Not Done Yet

* * *

On October 1st, 1976, I got offered a job working for SURFER Publications. At first, I worked for POWDER, which was the companies ski magazine, selling magazines to ski shops via phone. But then a position opened up at SURFER selling advertising. This worked really well for me because selling ads had a very flexible schedule that allowed me to surf when the surf was good and keep doing the music with the band. It also provided a much-needed regular income.

Not too long after that, I got a record deal for a single with Jet Records. Jet was the label for *Electric Light Orchestra*. They started a label for singles with us called Heavy Records. The A side was *"Skateboard Bill,"* which I had actually thought to be a children's record kinda song. The B-side was more of a surf rocker called *"Pocket Rocket."*

The band did a sort of transformation right about then. Jack Finn left the band and Richard Wilkens came in. Richard was a solid rock bass player and also doubled on Saxophone. This was a great addition having a horn sound to go with everything else and allowed us to stretch out a little bit and get away from doing all silly surf songs. When Richard played Sax I would switch over and play bass. Also, the *Corkettes* were really sounding good, and we started featuring them on a few songs of their own. At that time we changed our name from the *Funk Dog Surf Band* to the *Tropics*.

We got a manager who was working at KMET, the leading FM rock radio station in Los Angeles at that time, named Curt Danials. Curt was a great guy and believed in us and I think he really tried hard to get us gigs and helped to make this whole thing happen.

But the problem was that this was a band with a lot of people in it and the gigs we were playing, as cool and fun as they were, did not pay all that great. Nobody was making a living doing this and it was getting hard to hold it all together. I was so driven to make this work that I probably started pushing too hard. Make the songs better, practice more, all that. And that is really difficult when dealing with that many musicians.

Musicians are artists and each one has his or her own set of "things" to deal with. Get everybody to rehearsal on time, hahahaha.

Finally, one day it just kind of blew up. Working so hard and making no money was not going over very well with anybody and it became strained. Doug Miller was really the one to pull the plug, and rightly so. I was the front guy but he was the heart and soul of the band.

It had run its course and that was as far as it was going to go. So, we had a wake, and everybody went home still friends. It was sad, but it was necessary.

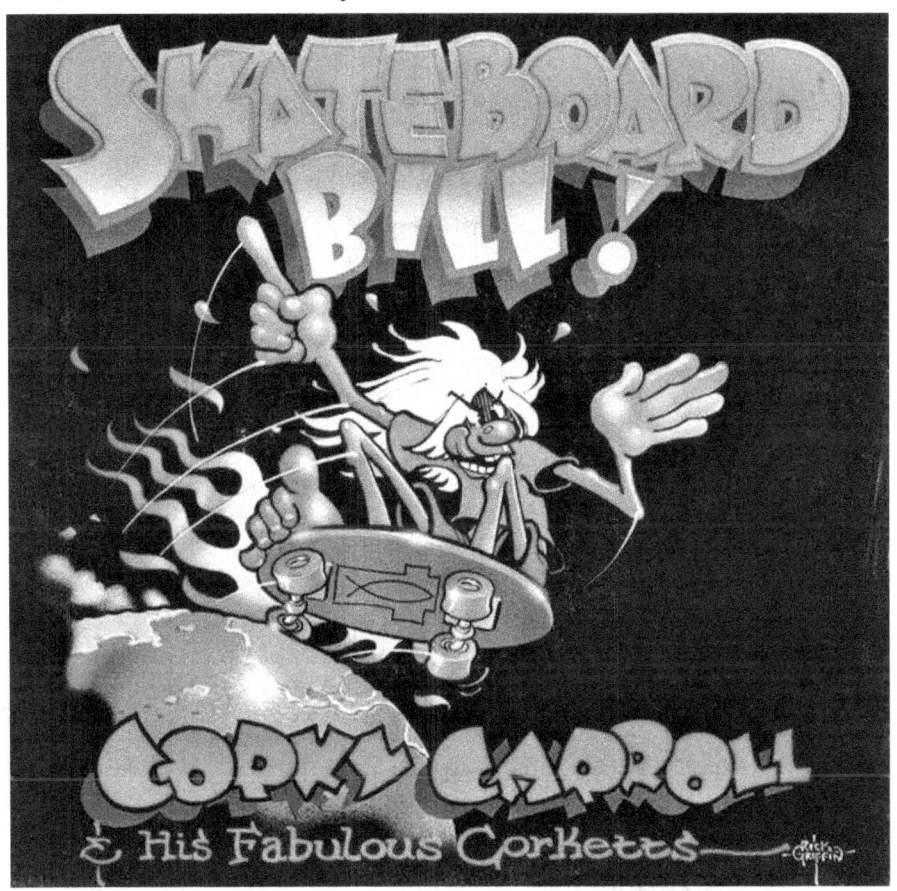

Cover of Corky's first single, SKATEBOARD BILL.
Done by legendary artist Rick Griffin.

CHAPTER 15

"*SURFER Magazine*"

Things were going very well for me at *SURFER Magazine* and within a short time, I got promoted to Advertising Director. This was an excellent job and one that I loved doing. We had an amazing staff of really talented, if not a little loco, people. I really liked all of them.

Steve Pezman was the publisher and big boss man. We had known each other since I was a little kid back in Surfside. He was one of the older dudes who came down from Long Beach and surfed at "Water Tower," just down the street from my house. He had driven Mark Martinson and myself many times on afternoon surf safaris to "Trestles," normally thanks to my mom coughing up the gas money. Sometimes Mark and I got stuck in the trunk of the car along with the boards, almost dying from the exhaust fumes. Steve also spent time on the North Shore and had ridden some big surf.

He was an established member of the surf community by the time John Severson hired him to take over the magazine when he sold it and moved to Maui.

About that time the whole surfing industry was in a sort of downward spiral and I honestly think John thought *SURFER* was going down with it and cast Steve as the captain that was going to go down with the ship. Pez, what everybody pretty much calls him, is a very talented dude and has a great eye for things. *SURFER Publishing* was sold to For Better Living Inc. This was owned by a talented businessman named Bud Fabian. The company consisted of *SURFER, POWDER* and *SKATEBOARDER* magazines.

I am pretty sure at first Pez was more than a little nervous about having me working there. He had known me all through my obnoxious early teen days when it was really difficult for me to not be motor mouthing constantly, probably one reason Mark and I got stuck in the trunk of the car so much on surf trips.

It wasn't hard to see that he was not sure how I was going to fit in. But I had somewhat grown out of having a constant "attitude" by then and was also very good at not only selling ads but also with organizing and managing the department. Within a short amount of time, I was able to turn things around and revenues were climbing and advertising bad debt was cut drastically. This was really a perfect job for me, and I loved it.

One day, maybe a year after the band had broken up, Rick Griffin came into my office. Rick was an incredible artist who had done Murphy cartoons in *SURFER* and then went on to become probably the leading artist in the San Francisco psychedelic period. He was doing album covers for the Grateful Dead and posters for concerts at the Fillmore and Golden Gate Park. He actually designed the lettering for the cover of *ROLLING STONE* magazine, and today that lettering is a "font" that people can buy and use.

We were pals and often traded babysitting duties, as our kids were about the same age. He brought in a guy named Chris Darrow because he thought the two of us should meet each other.

Chris is one of the great musicians of the world. He had been in the *Nitty Gritty Dirt Band* and the Kaleidoscope plus was the leader of Linda Ronstadt's touring band and had played with all kinds of famous rock and country bands.

Chris had just moved to San Clemente and was interested in learning how to surf. We became instant pals and started hanging out all the time. I got Chris a board, and we would go down to San Onofre in the afternoons and surf and have barbeques.

His girlfriend Carol and my Cheryl got along great, so we spent really a lot of time together. Chris started helping me with my music, encouraging me to branch out into playing more instruments and helping me with my singing. We were gurus to each other. I was his surf dude, and he was my music dude, it worked out very well.

After a while, we wrote some songs together and Chris arranged some of his pals to come down and put together a new band. These guys were all world-class studio type players and it really only took one or two rehearsals to be stage ready. Along with Chris and I, we had Chester Crill (who went by the name Max Budda) on electric violin and harmonica, Jerry Waller on piano, Paul Macri on Bass and John Russell on drums. We got the Corkettes back together in the form of Cheryl and Debbie and *"Corky Carroll and the Coolwater Casuals"* was born.

Right at that same time, my single *"Skateboard Bill"* was actually doing ok as far as getting some airplay and selling. Not setting the world on fire, but not crashing either.

A record company in England decided to release it over there and flew me over to do some promotions. I played them a tape of a new song that Chris and I had written and just recorded in my garage on my Teac 4 track tape recorder. It was called *"Tan Punks on Boards."* They loved it and wanted us to go into a studio and record it professionally.

Chris played it for his pal Mike Nesmith at around the same time. Mike had been a member of *"The Monkees"* and was a successful country musician. He also owned his own record company up in Carmel called Pacific Arts.

Mike liked it too and flew me up to have a meeting with him and sign a record deal for Tan Punks to be released in America on his label. He also came on board as producer.

We recorded the song at Lyon Studios in Newport Beach, along with a great tune called "From Pizza Towers to Defeat." Pizza Towers was written by a full-tilt crazy songwriter named Frizz Fuller.

Chris had invited Frizz to come to one of our rehearsals, thinking that he might be able to write a song or two for us. Three days later Frizz showed up with 77 songs. One of which was *"Tiki Torches at Twilight."* This became one of our regular kind of trademark tunes. Some years later David Lindley recorded it on one of his albums, and he and Jackson Browne started doing it live. Frizz was amazing. Pizza Towers became the B-side of the Tan Punks on Boards single.

Following that we recorded an entire album in my garage. It was titled *"Surfer for President."* Our piano player, Jerry Waller, wrote the song, Surfer for President, for me in light of the upcoming election and it became one of the opening songs to our set. Chris had a really cool ceramic blue tuna hanging in his kitchen, that we both liked, so we started *"Casual Tuna"* Records and released the Surfer for President album. With some ads in SURFER Magazine, we managed to sell the 1000 albums that we pressed.

We got booked to headline at the Troubadour in Los Angeles, a pretty important deal for that time period. Both Jackson Browne and Dennis Wilson, from the Beach Boys, showed up for the show. After we finished Dennis came backstage and said he loved us and wanted to help me.

He proposed producing an album for us in Brother Studios and getting us a record deal. Sounded great to me, and we make arrangements to get together and plan it out. Unfortunately, before this would happen Dennis drowned in an accident diving off of his boat in Marina del Rey.

This kind of put the wind outta my sails and was really sad. Not only to lose Dennis, but that big plumb of an opportunity just went out the window.

The "Corkettes," Corky and the Legendary Chris Darrow.
Headlining at the TROUBADOUR in West Hollywood
with the Coolwater Casuals.

Chris and I continued to play on and off in local restaurants and coffee houses as a duo but that night at the *Troubadour* was actually the last time the *Coolwater Casuals* ever played together again. Too bad, it was really a great band. But the music business is kinda cruel in a way. You can play in bars and make a small living doing it.

You can make it huge and play stadiums and make a huge living doing it. But get to the middle and it's really hard. The clubs pay better than bars, but you don't play every night.

You open concerts for bigger name acts and half the time you don't get paid at all. There is no money. And for an 8-member band, it's really hard. The band was always ready to play, but I was sort of losing my will to fight on trying to make it and getting content with my job at *SURFER*. I just sort of stopped looking for gigs.

Chris would eventually move back up to Claremont and I went into musical hibernation for about ten years.

***

SURFER was doing great. We moved into a bigger building in San Juan Capistrano, and I was able to expand my department. We were doing enough of the ad production for our clients ourselves that I was able to set up our own in-house advertising production department. I hired a killer young graphic artist named Mark Samuels. Between him, my assistant Denise Bashem, and I we were able to grow the revenue at a solid rate every year.

Denise was so good that Pez eventually moved her over to assist him with Publishing and to oversee the printing of the magazine. I got a new assistant named Michelle Jenkins, and we were working as a well-oiled machine. Cheryl was still working at Henry's and Clint was becoming a solid little surfer.

I will never forget the day when he was about six or seven years old. I had given him a yellow Doyle softboard. One day I was sitting on the beach at San Onofre with Dorian Paskowitz and Fred Van Dyke. We were all watching as Clint stood up, turned, and made a wave from take-off to the beach for the first time. Dorian matter of fact like commented, "Well, there goes college." Poor little dude just had too much of my DNA in him and would wind up following a life as a surfer/ musician just like his old dad.

Within a few years he really became a good surfer. I took him up to Hollister Ranch one time, and he just lit up Auggie's one afternoon.

Clint was hooked.

He hung out with the Paskowitz kids at San Onofre in the afternoons when we would do family barbeques, and he became a real surf rat beach kid.

CHAPTER 16

"The Great Disaster"

As things were going well for us financially at that time, we thought maybe it would be a good time to get our house put into my name, a little detail that we had sort of overlooked when I tuned 21. I had just been paying my dad every month and nobody ever seemed to think anything about it. So, I went to see my dad and told him that I wanted to go ahead and shift over the title now.

To my shock he totally freaked out. He was drinking really heavy by now. Him and my mom had divorced, and he was living with a girlfriend back in Surfside. He went into a rant about how having the house in his name was his only source of getting credit and if we changed it over he would be screwed and a whole line of verbiage that just didn't make a whole lot of sense. Basically, he said no, he wouldn't do it. This totally came out of the blue and we never saw it coming.

I didn't know exactly what to do, so I contacted a lawyer. It turned out that he had been charging me way more each month than the payments plus taxes and insurance really added up to. So he could claim that we only rented from him.

The only way I could get the house put into my name was to prove him mentally incompetent. He was an alcoholic for sure, but I both didn't think I could and didn't want to even think about trying to prove him mentally incompetent. We were stuck and it was an ugly mess.

This set a sad series of events into motion. One day a real estate guy came to the house and told us my dad had sold it and we had 30 days to vacate. I confronted him about it, and he was so drunk he could hardly stand up and his girlfriend told me to leave, or she was calling the cops.

We found a house to rent and moved out. He took all the money from the sale of the house, about 250 thousand dollars profit, retired from his job and left on a world cruise with his girlfriend.

We would never speak to each other again.

To make this horrible part of the story as short as possible: he went through almost all of the money and then shot himself in the head. He left what little he had left, about 20K, to me and left a motor home worth a lot more to his girlfriend. We were down at San Onofre one afternoon when Cheryl's brother Mike came down to tell us that he had killed himself. He had been at our house when the Seal Beach Police called with the news. To say that this was one of the darker days in my life would be a fact. I just went numb. Cheryl really went numb; in the long run I think it affected her even more than me.

We took the money he left me and put a down payment on a little wooden house on top of a hill in San Clemente. This was while Chris Darrow was still living there, and we were right down the street from him and Carol. Life went on and we just started over. But man, that was really a heavy blow.

CHAPTER 17

"Tennis and Beer"

When we moved into our new house in San Clemente one of the cool things was that there were two public tennis courts right around the corner and hardly anybody used them. As I was really into tennis and playing, what I thought was, quite a bit, these came in really handy. Only thing was that I never could find enough people to play with me. So I decided to get a bit more serious about it and I joined a very cool little tennis club in San Juan Capistrano called the "Capistrano Racquet Club."

One of the better decisions I made in life. This was the ideal place for my tennis desires to be fulfilled. The guy that ran the pro shop was one of the greatest players in the world on the senior circuit. He was in his fifties at the time and still was an incredible player and on top of that a totally cool dude. His name was Tony Prodan and he and I became instant pals. We used to have lunch together every day and then play a match right after, or the other way around.

In the beginning, he used to just work me and laugh about it. He was really good at lobs and drop shots and found it really fun to run me all over the court while he just stood there with his keys and change jingling in his pocket. As years went by and I got better, and he got older, it equaled itself out somewhat.

Tony had played big time tennis in the era of Bill Tilden and had been his doubles partner. He was pals with Poncho Gonzales and Bobby Riggs. We played doubles with those dudes and it was really a fun deal for me.

I learned more about Tennis from my daily matches and hanging out with Tony than I probably did from all the lessons and training that I did. I was totally hooked on the game and really focused on getting good at it.

Chris decided to move back to Claremont, where he was originally from, and I was on a break from music for the most part. It would be years until I got the bug again and started performing. I was pretty much just surfing, working at the magazine and playing tennis. Plus still managed to get in a ton of skiing in the winters.

Then, out of the clear blue sky, a real game changer came my way. I was in Hawaii surfing and visiting my clients that advertised in the magazine; I would do that once a year and line it up when the surf was good, and it wasn't real crowded. I used to stay with my pal Mark Martinson and his wife Jeanne. They lived right on the beach at Pupakea, near Pipeline, and Jeanne was an avid Tennis player. Ideal set up for me. I could surf, play tennis with Jeanne and take my clients to dinner. All part of the job. Did I mention I loved my job at SURFER?

One morning I got a call from a lady in New York that said she had been looking for me for two weeks and finally tracked me down. I was wanted in New York to read for a Miller Lite Beer commercial. Her name was Ellen, and she was from an agency called Blackman and Raber.

I thought somebody was playing a joke on me and looked out the windows to see if I could see any of the neighbors on the phone. Jeff and Patty Johnson lived next door with their three surfing sons, Jack, Trent, and Pete.

Jack would grow up and become the famous singer/songwriter Jack Johnson. I didn't see anybody on the phone, so I took her at her word. She asked if I could be in New York the next day. I said no. She said why not? I said there was a really good swell running.

She said when could I come? I said right after the swell goes down. She said to call her when the swell went down, and she would have tickets waiting for me at Honolulu airport. I said cool and hung up.

"What just happened?" I thought. Two weeks later I was in New York reading a script for a 30-second *Miller Lite* commercial. It was a cool script but a little bit not exactly the way that I would have said it. I mentioned that, and they let me read in more in my own words. They all nodded and said, "Cool, we will let ya know."

I flew back to California and went back to my daily routine not knowing if I got the gig or not.

* * *

A couple of months went by, and I was pretty sure that I had not got the commercial when the phone rang one afternoon. I was told to be at the Beverly Hills Hotel by 3 P.M. the next day for wardrobe and contract signing. Yep, I got the deal. I didn't even bother to ask how much I was going to make, I just figured whatever it was, it was gonna be something way more than I would have if I had not gotten it.

They shot the spot at a bar in Hermosa Beach called the *"Poop Deck."* I knew that bar; Dewey Weber hung out there a lot. In Dewey's later life, after he and his wife split up, he unfortunately did a lot of drinking and this was his hang out. It was the perfect beach bar for the commercial.

It went like this: I am walking through this crowded bar with lots of beach looking people hanging out. I say something like. "Yeah, all I ever do is hang out at the beach, surfing and groovin' on *Miller Lite*. It tastes great and has fewer calories than their regular beer."

As I say "groovin" I check out one of the chicks in the crowd. Then I go on to say, "Maybe it's time I made something of myself, maybe it's time I went out and got a real job?" A long pause, the whole crowd stops and there is no sound. Then I look at the beer, smile and give a big, "Nawwwwwww!"

It came out in the summer and was a hit; they wound up renewing the original 26-week contract for a second 26 weeks.

Corky in his first of several television commercials for MILLER LITE Beer. He was also a member of the famous MILLER LITE ALL-STARS

At that time a dude from *Miller Brewing Company* named Glenn Bougoius called me and set up a meeting in Los Angeles to talk about me being a part of the *"Miller Lite Allstars."* This was a group of about 25 of the retired athletes that were doing the *Miller Lite* commercials that *Miller Brewing* put under contract to do personal appearances all around the country.

This lineup included guys like Bubba Smith, Boog Powell, Red Auerbach, Dick Butkas, Billy Martin, Dave Cowens, Hacksaw Reynolds, Sam Jones, L.C. Greenwood, Burt Jones, Bob Ueker, Tommy Heinson and more.

My commercial had gone over really well with the younger age viewers, old enough to drink but like college age, and they wanted to aim me at that demographic. Naturally, I jumped at the chance to do this, not only would it be really fun but it paid very well. I would do Spring Breaks in Fort Lauderdale and Daytona, College Ski weeks all over the country and lots of other great fun events. And, get paid for it. Wow, what a concept.

* * *

As great as things were starting to go career-wise they were starting to go just as bad at home. Cheryl had continued to grow more fragile and had taken to seeing weird doctors with weird ideas. One guy insisted she do these constant colon cleanings, another insisted that she take thyroid medicine.

Turned out he was a thyroid medicine freak and prescribed it for everybody and anybody who came to see him.

She became a devout Christian and went to church and prayer meetings all the time.

Her sister Sheila married a guy who was a minister for Calvary Church and the three of them were constantly praying. Sometimes praying for me, which was probably a good thing actually. They tried to convert me many times, but I was stubborn.

I did, and do, believe in God. But I have never liked going to church and I really don't feel real comfortable talking about it. For me, God is a lot about what is right and what is wrong, but I don't have a particular religion that I feel I need to follow. It's just more personal. This was not a huge issue between us, but it was something.

But what really swung things in the wrong direction was when it came time for Clint to go to High School.

He had been going to a Christian school for the past few years and had been, for the most part, an average student. He wanted to go to San Clemente High School, so he could join the surf team.

When he went into 8th grade we told him if he got at least a B average that year we would let him go back to public school and enroll him at SCHS. Honestly, we never expected that he would, and we would have to. We wanted to keep him in a private Christian school, it was safer and offered a better education.

But the little rascal put his head down and worked hard and came out with a couple A's and the rest B's. We could not say no.

This was a horrible decision when looking back at it. As soon as he started school at San Clemente High School he fell in with both the right and wrong crowd. The right crowd because these guys were the top surfers. The wrong crowd because these dudes were also street savvy and were well into bad behavior, mostly smoking a lot of pot. As his freshman year went along we could see a change in him.

Cheryl didn't want to see it and sort of blinded herself to it. I wasn't really sure what to do about it.

His surfing was really good and he seemed happy, but there was a definite change in his moods and overall demeanor. He wasn't the same fun and happy kid. But then, he was a teenager and those years are really hard to figure out no matter who and what you are. I thought the best thing to do was just hope he didn't get into trouble and would be okay. Smoking pot wasn't the end of the world after all. I had certainly done it and I was just fine. Nonetheless, Cheryl started to get depressed and it was hard to get her out of it. The more weird doctors she got sucked into and the more Clint sort of drifted into whatever it was that he was drifting into, the more withdrawn and sadder she got.

During his sophomore year it all kind of hit the fan. He first got caught stealing a car and joy-riding. But then the capper was he got busted selling pot in the bathroom at school and got kicked out at the end of the year. He had been doing very badly in his classes and it was obvious that he was really on the wrong path.

He would do these bad things and Cheryl could not find it in her to punish him. He was her sweet little boy, and she didn't want to face the fact that he was NOT being a sweet little boy any longer.

Sadly, he was out of control. At least it seemed that way at the time, maybe it was him that was in control and it was us who were not. It's a little bit of a blur.

I was left to be the bad parent who had to hand out the discipline, something I was really not cut out for, nor good at.

An awful triangle formed in our household between the three of us. Clint would do something bad, I had to give him some sort of punishment (normally some sort of grounding) and Cheryl would cry and go into depression.

She would expect me to punish him, but it made her mad, sad and really unhappy when I did it. Plus, she could never be any kind of enforcer. I would put him on two weeks restriction, and he would come home from school and go surfing. If she tried to say anything he would just go anyway. Naturally, this would really upset her.

When I came home from work, she would be in tears. I know that when he got older he really regretted that, just as I have regretted a zillion things that I said or did when I was his age. At the time this made me really mad at him and the whole dynamic of our family went into a very horrible place. He would later say he did stuff like that, "because he could get away with it." The way things were he could and did. It all went from bad to worse, and then even more worse.

One day I actually smacked him one after he had mouthed off to his mom. This sort of shocked all of us. Something had to give, I didn't like being the bad guy and Cheryl couldn't. None of us were getting along with each other. I just hoped that somehow, someway, this would work itself out. I didn't see a way that it could, but I didn't know what to do.

I loved both of them and couldn't live with either at that moment. I was mad at Clint for doing what he was doing. I was sad, that I could not bring Cheryl out of her funk. Add to the fact, that me being the bad parent with Clint was splitting us up emotionally was making it worse and was driving me nuts. On top of that, Clint was just not getting it. He was gonna do what he was gonna do, no matter what we thought or wanted. He really didn't care.

Maybe he did, but the fact that it was so easy to get away with stuff made it so that he couldn't help himself, I don't know. I do know that inside he has a great heart and is a wonderful person. The time of life, his age and the way things were that were influencing him just took over and it was what it was. A real freaking bad mess.

One day I came up with a plan. I told Cheryl I would send her and her girlfriend, fellow Corkette Debbie, to Maui for an extended vacation. Basically, for as long as it took to clear her head and get out from under the massive depression that she had fallen into. I would rent them a condo and give them money to live on. All she had to do was not worry about anything and get better.

My pal Tom Castleton had become close with Clint and I thought could be a good influence on him.

Tom and his girlfriend came and stayed at our house and looked after Clint for a little bit. I had gotten him back into San Clemente High School, and my idea was to drop him off at school each day on my way to work. That way I would know he was going. I was going to try and be more of a pal to him and guide him back to a better attitude and way to do things. So, September started and the plan went into effect.

The first thing that happened is one of his buddies, that he had brought to our house, stole my very expensive camera. The one I needed to shoot ad photos for my job. This was not good. But it got worse, really fast.

On my birthday, September 29th, I was in the DMV in San Clemente renewing my driver's license. I walked out of the door at about 10 A.M. and was almost run down by Clint. He was on his skateboard with his surfboard under his arm and had quickly tossed away a joint he was smoking. The DMV office was on the way to the beach from our house.

He quickly and convincingly told me a story about how he did not have to be in school today because there was some sort of teacher conference going on and when he found out about it he got a ride home and was going surfing. He probably was hoping I had not seen the joint and did not mention it.

I wanted to believe him, but it was really hard too. Nonetheless, I let him go, I didn't want to call him a liar without knowing for sure if he was or wasn't telling the truth. I wanted to give him the benefit of the doubt.

I went home and called the school to check on his story.

Not only was I told that he was he supposed to be in school that day, but that he had never been in school at all since the semester had started a few weeks before. I had dropped him off every day, but he split without going to class. Yikes, this was bad.

But yes, it got even worse even faster. While I was sitting there in our kitchen, really Cheryl's kitchen, making a pot of coffee and trying to figure out what to do now, I got a call that changed everything.

A local drug dealer, who was a very bad guy, was on the phone. I knew this guy from surfing. He told me that Clint owed him $3000.00 for cocaine and that if he wasn't paid within a couple of days he would have no choice but to break Clint's legs.

He wanted to give me fair warning so I could have the chance to handle it one way or another. He said he was sorry about it, but it was what it was and he had no choice. Now this was really, really bad.

I was freaking out. How was I gonna fix this? I made some calls around asking about rehab centers and places that might be able to help. The one thing that was not good about that plan was that the person had to want to go, they could not be forced.

Then somebody told me about a place in Utah that was a locked reform school kinda place that dealt with this exact kind of situation. Grubby Clark had sent his son to it when he had been caught lighting cars on fire.

He had burned something like 30 cars before they caught him. He was going under the name "glow-worm."

I called Grubby and he told me that this place had been the answer for his boy and highly recommended it.

It was called Provo Canyon School. The deal was they sent a private plane down with two armed guards that would pick up Clint, by force if necessary, and take him back to Utah. He would be there a year, and they assured me that by that time they would have him "back on the right track." It was really expensive, but I did not see any better choice. It took pretty much all the money I had in the bank plus a huge monthly payment. If it could fix this problem then I was all in.

The next morning the two guys showed up at dawn and went to Clint's room to get him. He was asleep as well as one of his pals who was on the floor.

There was a big bag of pot and a pile of cash on the table. When these dudes burst in it took the boys by surprise, and they thought it was the police. Clint's pal jumped out the window and ran while the two guards took Clint out and down to their rental car.

While they explained to Clint what was happening to him, I got his suitcase with clothes and what he would need together and then took it down to say goodbye to him. THAT did not go well at all. He was livid and crying and screamed how much he hated me and how could I do this to him. I don't know how I could have ever been sadder than I was at that moment when they drove away. I was crying myself.

When I went back upstairs, my thought was that maybe I could use the drug money that was on his table to help pay off the dealer that he owed the 3k to. But his pal had snuck back in and taken the pot and the money. "Well, that figures," I said out loud.

I called Cheryl and told her what had happened. She just seemed down, and I think it was more than she wanted or needed to deal with at that moment.

They had only been over there about a month at this time. I just told her to relax and not worry about it.

He was in a safe place and I would take care of everything at home and all she had to do was heal and get herself feeling good again. No timeline and no pressure.

I didn't know it at that time but us getting back together was not meant to be.

After a while, we tried a couple of times, but things were not the same. It was strained and didn't feel natural. I had never thought that would happen.

During all those years we were together I really thought it was forever and could not even fathom a scenario where we would not be. But things happen and life changes and even though you don't want it to, it just does. This was one of those cases.

* * *

To this day I think Cheryl is one of the very best people that I have ever known. Her goodness is second to none. We had a wonderful marriage for 17 years, but it was over. When we both realized it we got a divorce. The good thing is we did not end up as enemies or anything like that. I look back on my time with her as one of the very good parts of my life. A big part of the reason that it was so good was because of her and not me. She was the better one.

* * *

Working at *SURFER* gave me the chance to meet and become friends with many people in the surfing industry that I probably would not have really gotten to know otherwise. One of them was Balsa Bill Yerkes. Bill ran a popular surfwear company called *Sundek*. I had known him a little bit from surfing events on the east coast in previous years, but it was from our working relationship through *SURFER* that we really became close pals.

I designed and produced a number of ad layouts for him in the mid- 80s. Every year he held a big surfing contest in Florida at the Holiday Inn in Melbourne Beach, and I became the M.C. for these events, which went by the name *"The Sundeck Classic."*

There was good surf right in front of the hotel, and the hotel provided a perfect place for everybody to stay, and for staging the event. I am not sure if this was a bigger surfing event or bigger out- and-out party. Either way, it was a really cool and fun thing and I had a great time.

At one of these *Sundeck Classics*, I remember watching Kelly Slater winning the little kids division, the 12 and under or something like that. He was probably the best surfer in the entire contest even at that age. When I was announcing that final heat I remember saying to the crowd, "this kid is gonna become World Champion one day, remember that you heard it here first." I am not sure how many people that were there remember that, but it certainly turned out to be a fact, eleven times over.

Balsa Bill and I had a lot in common. He was sort of a surfing historian and also a dam good musician. We spent a lot of time together and somewhere along the line we started talking about the possibility of Sundek producing a "designer" line of surfwear, a bit more upscale than what he was doing.

I had some ideas, and he had some ideas and in the middle of all that the idea of "Corky" surfwear was hatched and was being mulled over by both of us. The job at *SURFER* was good, but this might have much greater possibilities for me in the long run if it took off.

CHAPTER 18

"Surfwear and Buckwheat"

Sometime in the year after Cheryl and I had split up I met Audrey Jean Gomez. She was a pretty and really fun local girl that was the daughter of a Mexican Blackfoot Indian named Clancy and an Irish mother named Jimi-Rey. She had two brothers, Gary and Jon, and a sister named Carla who all were light skinned like their mama. Audrey had beautiful dark skin she got from her dad. A wonderful family that I liked immediately. Her sister was married to a cool dude named Jim Lowrey, who Audrey liked to call "Mr. Lowrey."

One night at dinner she said something to him like, "pass the butter Mr. Lowrey." To which he replied, "O.K. Buckwheat." I cracked up and from that moment on she was no longer Audrey, she was Buckwheat. Many of my friends who met her only know her as Buckwheat as that's all we ever called her.

Today this would probably be very politically incorrect, everything is. But there was nothing bad meant at all, it was just so delightfully perfect.

As fate would have it, we met in a local bar and started seeing each other.

She was really fun to be around and would always make friends with everybody, no matter where we were. Like, if we were on a bus, by the end of the ride we knew everybody and had dinner plans with half of them. She had a great spirit and was a dedicated party animal.

Right about then I was ready to just have fun and pull myself out of the funk that I had sort of settled myself into.

Working at *SURFER* in those days was a lot of fun due to the amazing and crazy staff we had. The Moe brothers over in the *POWDER* section, all the crazies at *SKATEBOARDER*, Tom Servais, Jeff Devine, Art Brewer on the photo and darkroom staff, Bob Bailey in the storeroom (always good for a prank), Dana Gordon, Debbie Bradley (later to marry Pez and start *SURFERS JOURNAL* together) and a bunch more group of fun people. It was kinda like a big family in a way. We had one chick that worshiped Eric Estrada and another who was in love with O.J. Simpson, to the point where she actually had a birthday party for him every year in his honor. I wonder if she still does that?

* * *

Things were going well and each year we were more successful financially than the last. It was a good place to be at right then, but the idea of having my own line of surfwear was really gaining my interest. Buckwheat was kinda fanning that flame too as she was way more into current fashion and what was cool, than I had been up to that point. She kinda aimed me toward dressing better, or at least more hip I guess would be the word. And I started paying attention.

I was also getting deeper and deeper into playing tennis, it had become an obsession just like surfing.

The good part about my schedule at the magazine was that for the most part, I didn't have one.

The job was to sell all the ad space and collect the money, and as long as I was doing that I could pretty much work on my own time frame.

When the surf was good I found a way to be there. Sometimes taking clients with me or going to visit them and surfing in their area with them. This was a good perk of the job.

I think it bothered Pez sometimes when I would roll in at 10 or 11 with wet hair and beaming over the clean swell that was hitting and that I had just had a go at that morning. But I was doing the job well, so he just flowed along with it.

It didn't occur to me that he might be feeling the same way that Jim Gilloon had felt back in the days when I was working for Hobie and would screech in around noon in my Porsche with my board on the roof, get paid more than what he was making, happily hoot at everybody and screech back out.

* * *

Somehow for most of my life, I have been able to find a way to work at my own pace, so I could do the stuff I wanted to do no matter what it was that I was doing. And normally I was pretty successful with whatever it was. And normally I didn't really realize that other people who were working with me or around me might not like it. This proved to be the case many times. I am not saying that this was the case at *SURFER*, but there could have been a little vibe there that either I didn't see or just did not want to see.

Then one day my good friend Allan Seymour warned me that this might be the case and to watch my back.

It seemed a bit weird because I was delivering not only what was expected of me but considerably more than that, year in and year out. It felt a little bit unfair, but then that is the way things happen sometimes.

* * *

So there it was, the signal to move into the next phase in my life. Balsa Bill, who owned Sundek, had made me an offer to come and work with him doing the CORKY line. This would include surfboards as well as clothing.

My job was to design the line and also put together the advertising. To start out with I would be making about the same as I had been at SURFER, maybe a little less.

The potential was there to make considerably more if the line was successful. Also, this really freed up my time to surf and play tennis.

I was also getting really busy doing appearances for Miller Lite and doing more television commercials. This appeared to be a really good career move and I was really stoked about it.

Exactly ten years to the day from when I had been hired, on Oct 1, 1986, I left my job at *SURFER* and went to work with Balsa Bill..

Bill and I went about buying material from Hoffman Fabrics and then going to Ohio to the factory, where Sundek was made, to design the patterns and get the line together. It was a fun and learning experience.

I will never forget one thing that happened on one of my Miller Lite appearances right around that time. They used to do Miller Lite All Star cruises on Norwegian Cruise Lines in the spring and fall every year. Miller would send 4 of us at a time on one of these cruises, and we could do two a year. I loved them and always took part in those promotions. We were also allowed to take wives or girlfriends with us.

On this one particular cruise Buckwheat had gone with me and one morning when we had just pulled into Antigua. We were walking down the hallway to debark the ship when we heard a radio in somebodies' cabin. It was mentioning President Bush and Magic Johnson and it sounded like one of them had gotten HIV.

I had been a devout LAKERS fan since my days working with Jerry West and to this day I bleed purple and gold.

I remember that moment clearly and saying to Buckwheat, "God, I sure hope it's Bush."

Now don't get me wrong, I wished nothing bad on President Bush. This was the older one by the way.

It's just that Magic Johnson is my all-time hero and I loved him and the way he played during the "Showtime" era of the Lakers. One thing I regret in life is so far I have never met him, I always wanted to because I worship the dude.

When it turned out that it was him, and he was going to have to stop playing, I totally broke down and cried. How could this be? Magic Johnson? That big ol' smile and happy dude coming down the court setting up some unbelievable play, Big Game James Worthy on one wing and Michael Cooper on the other with Kareem following behind. You knew something wonderful was gonna happen, you just didn't know what. And then it did. This was just horrible news and I took it hard.

One of my other duties for the All Stars was to do the college ski weeks. I was the only one that skied other than Burt Jones, and he had broken his neck playing football, so he was pretty limited to what he could do skiing wise. Sometimes they would send both of us, and also L.C. Greenwood. LC. didn't ski, but he was a wonderful dude to have along, totally coolster to the max. He could sing "Wild Thing" better than anybody. But most of the time I was sent solo. I would go to Aspen, Steamboat Springs, Crested Butte and a number of other top ski resorts around the country.

My job was to ski wearing a Miller Lite All Stars parka and after skiing hit a couple of bars where I would toss out a bunch of Miller Lite hats, yell out "Tastes Great," to which the entire bar would yell back, "Less Filling!"

Then I would buy a round of Miller Lite for everybody, sign some posters and move on to the next bar. It would be about an hour in each bar and we normally did two or at the most three each day. The best part was they actually paid me to do this, really paid me well at that. How good was this???

Right about then Scott Funk and Dave Clark had opened a surfing retreat on a little island in Fiji called Tavarua. The word was, this place had some of the best lefts in the world, and I did love going left. I would go on one of those extended ski trips for Miller and come home to a big fat check waiting for me.

This would immediately transform itself into airplane tickets and an extended surf trip to Tavarua. Did I mention that I have never been great at saving money or "putting something away for a rainy day?"

***

This was a time in my life that I was mostly ignoring the fact I was getting older and might want to plan for the future. I was making money and turning it into instant fun. The future would take care of itself when it became time. But right then I was just riding on the freedom I had and the fact that I could do these things.

I was also spending a lot of time surfing down at Puerto Escondido, on the southern coast of Mainland, Mexico. I loved that spot. Big, heavy, gnarly, bone-crushing barrels to go along with warm water, and you could stay there really cheaply.

Between Puerto and Tavarua I was getting a lot of great surf adrenalin thrust through my system.

A huge chunk of what I was starting to make had been going to cover Clint's stay at Provo Canyon School. I was also sending money to Cheryl each month as part of our alimony agreement.

So the fact was I was not really rolling in cash, but what there was of it I was not holding on to. Skiing, surfing, tennis, and adventures with Buckwheat.

When Clint got out of Provo they set him up to live in a sort of halfway house with a minister and his family who lived in nearby Dana Point. The idea was he would work his way back into normal society and then be able to move back home with me. The hope was that he had been rehabilitated and everything would be O.K.

But, noooooo. Within a couple of weeks he was caught selling pot to the minister's son and sleeping with his daughter.

Looking back on it now I almost have to laugh about it, but at that time it was not very funny.

It was obvious that he was still out of control, or... depending on which side of the deal you were on, He was traveling on a path that only he could see as being viable.

He wound up staying with friends and embarking on about twenty years of getting in and out of trouble, going to jail, almost making it in music but going back to jail instead.

Becoming a great surfer and musician and not being able to get out from under his addiction.

I don't even know what he was all into, but it was a very bad road that he traveled for a long, long time. I always loved him but tried to keep him at arm's length because the things he was doing would be bad for me if they spilled over into what I was doing. I would loan him money when he asked for it and try to be a pal to him, but as a father, I was not much good. He scared me really. He could be very intense.

It was really a bummer that the year Clint spent in Utah had done no good, other than to just keep him off the streets for that amount of time.

In many ways, he and I are a lot alike. We both want to do what we want to do and are willing to go the extra mile to make it happen the way we want it too. His love for surfing and music are just the same as mine, we share both of those things in common.

We are both hard headed and not all that compromising either. I wanted him to stop using drugs and he didn't want to. This led to many unhappy moments between us.

Thank God, that in later years he came around and totally made himself over, a thing I could never express as to how proud I am of him in mere words.

His inner goodness and heart finally found a way out and he has worked through all sorts of trials and hardships to get himself together and make a life for him as well as his son, Cannon. More on this later.

* * *

The first year of the clothing line things went fairly well, and during the second year, I got more involved with actually going out and making some sales.

The biggest deal I made was to have my line in a chain of stores called Miller's Outpost. This had nothing to do with Miller Brewing Company.

They tried us out in a few stores and we sold really well. So the next year they ordered big for all of their 180 something stores.

The numbers from this one account alone would put me on the map and assure the immediate success of the line.

Things on that end seemed, at least on the surface, to be going very well.

* * *

Things were not going all that great with Buckwheat and I though. Did I mention she was a dedicated party animal? Well, she was.

Things would happen, like I would give her money to go to the store to buy something for dinner.

She wouldn't come back for a few days and when she did she would be pretty dog-eared, and worse for wear and tear. And not have any food to show for it either.

I would be angry, and she would be sorry, and we would break up.

Somehow she would look at me with her big beautiful eyes, maybe a tear or two coming down her cheek, and cuddle up next to me saying goodbye. I would cave, and all would be forgotten until it happened again. I am not sure how I should have handled that situation. I didn't want to lose her, but this was a crazy way to live at the same time.

We took off for a long stay on Tavarua in May, I am pretty sure it was 1989. I was kind of hoping we would have a wonderful time and everything would be cool.

Even though we did have a wonderful time there was damage done and the writing was on the wall, it had been a fun and wild ride with Buckwheat and I always think of her with a smile. We were just on different paths.

On top of that, I was totally blindsided when we got home to find out that Sundek had crashed while we were gone.

Without going into details, fabric had never been ordered and the factory was contracted to build all the gear and couldn't do it without the fabric. The offices were closed and Bill wasn't answering his phone.

I was never really clear on what had happened to make that all come down, but it did. So, with no warning, I was out of a job.

The Miller's Outpost guy was calling me wondering where all the goods he had ordered were and was he not happy. It actually took a few days just to find out that the company was closed down, and when I did it was just kinda numbing.

Poof, just like that. No job, no girlfriend, humph!!!

On the island of Tavarua in Fiji with Chief Druku and Surfer/Scientist/Pedal Steel player Bob Siggins.
Photo: Buckwheat Gomez.

CHAPTER 19

"Tennis and Cars"

In the aftermath of the loss of the clothing line income, I started teaching tennis. I had worked my way up through the ranks and was a competent player by that time, good enough to work as a teaching pro. This, along with appearances for Miller was keeping me afloat financially. I also did some work helping design a line of surfing wetsuits for a company from Canada called "Bear." They were big in water-skiing and wanted to tap into the surf market, so they hired me to help them do that.

I had what I thought was a great idea in the form of a lightweight water sock that had a sole that would protect your feet from rocks or whatever, have grip and yet be light and easy to wear. Anybody who went to the beach could use these. They thought it was a stupid idea and shot it down.

A year and a half later Nike came out with the Aqua Sock and sold like 900 zillion of them. They didn't really make a serious enough commitment to surfing and so that gig only lasted about a year.

* * *

I was pretty happy just surfing, plus teaching and playing tennis. Miller was keeping me busy with appearances and doing commercials.

I was trying to find other forms of income but wasn't really coming up with much. Then one day I got a call from an old surfing friend from the 60s named Malcolm McCassey. He had been one of the better surfers in the North County of San Diego area and also had surfed in many of the early surfing contests in California.

He was the General Manager of a number of car dealerships in Orange County and I guess one of them, which was located in San Juan Capistrano, was not doing as well as they expected it to do. It was a Honda and Jeep dealership located right off the freeway very close to my tennis club. Malcolm knew that I was pretty business savvy from my years at SURFER and was a good salesman. What he was looking for was a mole to go in and figure out why the dealership wasn't doing well.

He offered me the job to go in as a salesman and report back to him anything I could find out that might get business stronger than it was. It came with a guaranteed income against whatever I would make from sales. Now I have to admit that I never saw myself as a car salesman. In fact, it had never ever once entered my mind as something I might ever be doing. But the offer was good, and I wasn't doing anything else, so I figured "why not."

I don't really want to go into great detail about this little venture, so I will make it as short as possible. I met some really cool people and also learned a ton about that kind of business.

For about six months I did sales, and was by far the leading salesperson they had, and also gave reports and suggestions to Malcolm on how to increase business.

Then they made me a sales manager at a little car leasing store they had inside the Mall in Mission Viejo, one of the most boring things I ever did. After about eight months I couldn't take it any longer and decided that was not the job for me.

I look back at that whole thing and chalk it up to getting some useful education and some useful income, but not the highlight of my life.

One thing that did come from my time at the car dealership was meeting a girl named Pamela Hastings. She was the friend of Michele Conception, who was our receptionist. One night after work a bunch of us went out for drinks at a bar in the Dana Point Harbor and Michele brought Pam along.

It was one of those "one thing led to another" and within a very short amount of time, we became a couple. She had a good job working at the Allan Cadillac dealership in Mission Viejo.

* * *

After leaving the car business, I devoted myself pretty much full time to teaching tennis. I went to work for a company that managed a number of tennis facilities in Orange County. At first I just taught at one of them in Laguna Niguel, but eventually started working at more of them and took over as their head pro. I was still surfing but tennis was taking up most of my time.

One of my favorite things in my tennis career was that I was invited to play in many "celebrity" tournaments for charities all around the country. It was at one of those events, in the friendly town of Billings, Montana, that this little interaction took place.

This particular event involved both, a tennis and golf tournament and included a huge list of invited celebrities. On the Friday night before the tennis and golf events started they held a big softball game between the "Hollywood All Stars" and the local softball team.

I thought it was gonna just be a little fun event, but noooo. Turns out they sold out a 10,000-seat minor league baseball stadium for this, and it was on local television.

I see this and am thinking, seeing as how there are dozens of bigger names here for this than me, I doubt I will have to play.

So, I am sitting in the dugout, trying to look invisible, when Rod Dedeaux comes rolling in. Rod was the baseball coach at U.S.C. for years and was also my neighbor when I was growing up in Surfside. He is coaching the Hollywood All Stars. He sees me and goes, "Coorrrky, I heard you were here. Great, you will be my leadoff hitter."

Oh no, this is not good. I am watching this dude warming up on the mound tossing up these 14' to 16' foot high pitches that are twisting and doing all this stuff and landing right on the plate every time, it was THAT kind of softball.

I go into semi-panic mode and am thinking of how bad it would look if I boogied on outta there right then. But, as fate would have it, in strolls Joe DiMaggio. Mr. Coffee himself, right there in front me. So, I seized the opportunity and innocently say, "Hey Joe, I need your help. I am just a dumb surfer/tennis player and I have never seen, nor tried to hit, a pitch like that. How do you hit that?"

On that note, the entire dugout does an "E.F. Hutton," and stops dead. Everybody is waiting to hear what Joe has to say. And there were some huge sports guys in there such as Ahmad Rashad, Kenny Anderson and Rick Berry.

Joe pauses and looks down at me sitting there, considering his words carefully. And very direct and sincerely he says, "Corky, I am gonna tell you how to hit that pitch. But I am going to tell you this one time and one time only, so listen carefully."

I am listening super carefully and so is everybody else in there, I can't believe I am actually getting a batting tip from Joe DiMaggio. This would be like some kook from Pasadena getting a surf tip from Duke Kahanamoku.

After a short pause, for effect I think, he slowly and firmly tells me, "KEEP...YOUR EYE....ON.....THE BALL!"

Oh yeah, of course. It had to be that. I would tell people that all day long when giving them tennis lessons.

"Keep your eye on the ball, relax, bend your knees and follow through." The grail. Everybody kinda gives an "oh yeah," and goes back to doing what they were doing.

When they were announcing me as leading off for the Hollywood All Stars I was shaking and sweating bullets. The pitcher, who had a handlebar mustache and looked amazingly like Rollie Fingers was confidently sizing me up.

This was worse than close out sets on a giant day at Waimea Bay.

I went up and swung as hard as I could at the first pitch, closing my eyes in the process, resulting in a zillion foot high pop up to the pitcher. When I came back in the dugout Joe says, "Well, you hit it."

* * *

In March 1991 Pam and I decided to get married. She was a lot of fun and we seemed to fit together pretty well.

After the wild and crazy ride with Buckwheat, something much more stable and down to earth seemed like the thing I was hoping for at that point in my life. The party animal in me was now pretty well tamed down, and I was thinking that a nice peaceful life with a partner I could count on would be just the ticket.

We got married by a dude in a magician outfit at one of those places in Las Vegas. I remember thinking that this thing was so hokey that it couldn't possibly be binding. Just in case it didn't work out I was probably safe.

Later that year we found out that Pam was pregnant. At first, I was kind of in shock. We had not planned to have kids. I was already pretty old for that, and already had Clint.

But, when she had an ultrasound and I saw this tiny baby girl
in there, I just melted and that was that. I loved her from that moment on.

***

My mom was not doing all that well with her health about that time. She had diabetes, and cancer in one of her eyes.

She wound up having to have her eye removed and was having a hard time getting around. She told me that she was going to move out to Arizona with my half-sister Norma, who would look after her.

***

Pam had never really liked living in my house in San Clemente because it had been Cheryl's house and she said she never felt comfortable there.

I had paid off that place long before, so we were able to kinda start off fresh without a ton of overhead.

We moved into the townhouse where my mom had lived in Huntington Beach, and got ourselves set up for the birth of Kasey Chanelle Carroll in June 1992.

CHAPTER 20

"Huntington Beach"

I have to admit that moving back to the Huntington Beach area from South Orange County was a big change. The San Clemente area was much quieter and even though the surf spots were crowded, they were a lot mellower. The surf pack at the Huntington Beach Pier is, for lack of a better word, intense.

When I first started surfing the pier again, after a lot of years away, it was a shock over how aggressive it was out there and how hard it was to fit into the pack and get any waves. There was absolutely no respect for age and experience or anything like that, it was dog eat dog and don't even think about showing up if you were a cat.

I was riding mid-sized boards, in the 7-foot range, which was what I had been on since the mid-1970s. At the pier there were the young hot guys on under 6' shortboards, who ruled the place. Then there was a pretty good-sized crew of older dudes on longboards who were able to get waves just because they were on big boards, even if this did annoy the hot young guys.

There was a sort of co-existence that was not based so much on comrade as it was out of that was just the way it was and there was no way around it other than to just accept the fact even if you didn't like it.

As a slightly overweight old dinosaur EX whatever on a mid-size board, I didn't have a connection with either group and was left to fend for myself the best I could. Plus, there was also the fact that I had been spending much more time playing tennis than I had been surfing and I would have to say my surfing skills were at the lowest level of my life.

It's 25 years later as I am writing this, and I am, well, 25 years older. I can honestly say I am surfing better now than I was then. So, long story short, I was having a really hard time fitting in with that crew.

At first, I just didn't surf there much. When I did surf I would drive south to San Onofre or Cotton's Point. Also, I was taking a yearly trip to the Island of Kauai about then, I always loved that place. Tennis was talking up most of my time anyway.

But then one day I was in the Windansea Surf Shop buying a leash or something and met the owner. A feisty redheaded Irish dude named Jack Flynn. We kind of hit it off and in talking to him he asked me if I needed a job. I was pretty well booked up with tennis lessons, as it was summer, but I told him I wouldn't mind working in the shop on Sundays. The extra income would help with Kasey just being born and also would sort of lure me back into surfing more and finding my way into the new order that had taken over the town since I had been around in the 60s.

* * *

Pam had gone to work for a cosmetics company in Laguna Hills right about the time we had gotten married.

Not long after Kasey was born they decided to move the company to Phoenix, Arizona. She had a good position in the company and really wanted to stay with them.

For a short time we actually considered moving out there so she could keep her job.

I had my teaching credential with the United States Professional Tennis Association and figured I could probably get a good job at a tennis or country club out there. But, what about surfing?

This was a really weird kinda decision and position to be in. I was, am, always have been and always will be a surfer first and foremost. Even if at that particular time my surfing was at an all-time low for both skill and time in the water, it was still who I was.

As tempting as the whole thing was financially, there was just no way I could see myself living in the desert hundreds of miles from the beach. So, we passed on that.

Fall came and tennis lessons were dropping off, Jack offered me the job of managing his surf shop full time. I could set the schedule so I could still keep my tennis job and run the shop too. It wasn't a ton of income, but we could scrape by for the time being.

In order to be able to get at least a few waves when I was surfing at the pier I started riding longboards again. This was good in the fact that at least I could surf out there without getting totally shut out by both the long and shortboard crews. It was bad in that it kind of set my already not so progressive surfing back a step or two. Honestly I never really felt that I fit in all that much when I was surfing the pier with anybody other than close pals.

I remember one afternoon in particular that a little incident occurred that sort of summed it all up for me. The surf was small but fun and the normal pack of surf rats were out there battling for every hint of a wave that came along. I had been sitting in the lineup for quite some time trying my best to snag one when a nice little peak came in. I was the only one right in the perfect spot to take off.

As I was paddling into the wave one of the younger hot dudes, who was paddling out, turned and paddled right in front of me almost causing me to run him down as I was about to stand up. He barely got himself around me and turned around and took off right behind me. This was what you would call a total "snake" job.

I was already in the wave and turned off the bottom hard and went up the face of the wave and hit the lip and fell off. My board almost hit the kid but didn't. I got on my board and started to paddle back out. I turned around to see if the kid was okay, not intending to say anything about it other than maybe, "are you okay?" He had snaked me and was the one in the wrong, but at the pier, it was dog-eat-dog, as I said. This kind of thing was the way it was now done, all the time, so I was just gonna keep my mouth shut.

However, the kid was pissed off and gave me some hand gestures. This in turn pissed me off, and I of course said something back. It wasn't a major deal really, just one of those things.

For me, it kind of set the tone for my dealings with the younger, much more aggressive, surf crowd at the pier. It was like, "hey, I was here first. Give me a break." For them it was like, "You had your time, now it's ours." And, to be honest, they were right.

The Huntington Beach Pier is not your normal surf spot. It's ground zero for the latest in state of the art surfing, a proving ground if you will. Everything I had to prove had been done decades before. I was an old Buick on a Formula One track.

* * *

Then one day Miller Lite invited all the Allstars to Milwaukee for a banquet. It turned out to be a farewell party of sorts. They had turned the advertising campaign over to a new agency and it turned out that they could not continue with the "Tastes Great, Less Filling" campaign, and the Allstars, any longer due to the fact that the old agency owned the rights to that campaign.

So that was the end of that, and they called us all in to say thanks and goodbye and all that haba sababa.

It was a kind of a shock to most of us, some were angry about it and some just took it like it was what it was and were thankful for the years that it was happening. I was very thankful, but really wished that it was not over.

Miller Brewing Company had been very good to me over the years and had been one of the best things that really ever came my way. I was gonna miss hanging out with the crew, Ueker, L.C., Burt, Bubba, Red, Cowens, Hacksaw, Madden, Billy, Sam Jones and the rest.

It had been a great run though, and one that I will always look back on as a gift.

* * *

Then a few good things happened for both Pam and I about the same time. She got a job at Tiempo Escrow, whose office was only a block from our house.

It was an entry-level position but had good hours and lots of room to advance. One thing about Pam is that she was always a very hard and dedicated worker and when she put her mind to it she could do big things. So this was an opening that fit her perfectly.

For me, it was that music stuck its melodic head back into my life. I got an offer from a small record label in Switzerland to put out a "Best of" album from all my old recorded songs. It came as a surprise! And they asked if I wanted to do a new one. Bigger surprise! I had not been playing for a long time and had no new songs ready to go. But, this got my interest going again and I went for it.

Before long I started doing solo gigs in local coffee houses and bars.

I did a show opening for somebody at the Lighthouse in Hermosa Beach, a respectable gig, and it went very well. This was enough to inspire me to start writing songs again and try to construct a little act.

Then I got a call from a guy at the Orange County Register newspaper saying they were looking for somebody to write a surfing column for the Huntington Beach Wave, which was the local paper and an insert into the Orange County Register. Peter Townend had recommended me for the job. He asked if I could send them a column so they could check out my writing.

I did, and they liked it, and I got the gig for a column a week. It didn't pay much, but I really enjoyed doing it.

Cool thing was that it got popular pretty fast and soon I was offered another column in the main paper, on the front page of the Local section.

This would eventually lead to a third column which was a question and answer piece in the Sports section. Add it all up and it was a nice little monthly aid to our financial situation. Cool thing is that I am still writing these, some 25 or so years later, it's still going strong.

I have been expecting it to end, but thankfully it keeps going and I hope it does for a long time still. I really like doing it.

Peter "PT" Townend, David Nuuhiwa and Corky.
Photo: Raquel Sauza Carroll.

* * *

Another thing happened that really would have a big impact on my life, I just didn't know it at the time.

Some years back, I had done a sports talk show with a dude named Rick Walker, and a month or so after that his daughter turned up in one of my tennis classes.

One night when Rick was picking her up he, sort of surprised like, asked me what I was doing teaching tennis. He said I should be teaching surfing. I told him I had been doing tennis for a long time and there was work doing it. As far as I knew there was very little work teaching surfing. This was before the big surf school boom.

A few weeks later he showed up at the surf shop with the idea that he and I open a surfing school in Huntington Beach.

It sounded kinda crazy and like a lot of work to put together, but I had nothing to lose by saying, "Sure, you put it together and I'm in." I honestly thought that would be the end of it.

But no. A month or so went by and Rick shows back up and tells me we are all set to go. He had gotten permits for Bolsa Chica State Beach, had some boards made, bought insurance, and we were set to open in June, a couple of months from then.

I was in shock, the dude really did it.

So, I drew up a logo and started thinking about how to set up the lessons and all that. Rick was probably an intermediate surfer at best, so the first thing was to coach him up and get him tuned in.

By opening day we had a few good instructors hired and were ready to go. And it worked. We didn't make much money that first summer, but the groundwork was laid and it was ready to grow.

Rick really put his heart and soul into it. I decided that this was really more his deal than mine, and he was doing all the behind the scenes stuff, so we worked out a deal where he would own the school although it would have my name on it, and I would get some money for it. For the next several years my part would be showing up to say a few words each week, do private lessons and be the figurehead. Rick took care of all the rest. The school really took off.

CHAPTER 21

"Not A Good Wipeout"

1996 was not the greatest year I ever had physically. Things were going pretty much O.K. until they didn't.

Pam was working her way up in the Escrow business. I was doing pretty good with both the tennis and managing the surf shop.

Then, sort of out of the blue, problems developed.

The first thing that happened was I stretched my Achilles tendon playing tennis one morning. In the blink of an eye my tennis life was over, just like that. My doctors told me if I continued to play I would snap it and have to have surgery, which also might end my surfing too.

It was a bummer for sure, but the choice was obvious. Keep playing and possibly end both my tennis and surfing careers or give up tennis and keep surfing. It was adios tennis and more time back in the water surfing.

To this day I miss being on the court, but it was not worth the risk of not surfing.

Music was once again, finding its way back, and taking more of my time.

Pam didn't really support my lifestyle a whole lot when it comes right down to it. She never considered things like surfing and tennis were a real way to make a living and had many times suggested I go out and get a "real job."

I always asked her, "didn't you see the freaking commercial?" This was referring to my first Miller Lite commercial where I say, "All I do is surf and hang out at the beach and maybe it was time I went out and got a real job? (Pause, think about it) Nawwwwww."

It wasn't a real debate. She had met me when I was working at the car dealership, so she just never got the fact that I was who I was and did what I did, she was thinking a 9 to 5 that brought in a real salary. I never got the idea she was real keen on my music either. "It's too mellow, you need to up the tempo." In retrospect I think back and she was probably right.

In recent years, and more from the advice of my current wife Raquel than anything else, I have changed my whole show to more solid rock and very few slow songs at all, and it has worked very well.

Back then I would write songs about things like falling asleep. Honestly, I did. I had this one song that I loved called, "I'm fading out." It was actually about falling asleep. She hated it and suggested I never play it again. So, I never did, at the time I thought it was. a cool song.

Anyway, the point is that although we had a nice life and got along very well it was true that we were not exactly on the same wavelength on some things.

Pam was really ambitious, almost fanatically so. I admired that about her and thought back to my days coming up as a surfer and also my early years in music. I wanted to succeed very badly. That was the way she was and I thought it was great.

At this point in my life I just did not have that same fire to conquer the world. There was a pretty big age gap between us and she had the zing of youth while I was settling nicely into middle age.

I was pretty happy to ride some waves, play some music and get by with what income I could make in the surf shop, my columns and with an occasional T.V. commercial.

The commercials paid really well and would often come at just the right time when we were really low on money.

In my mind things were just fine, but she always wanted more. And when she wanted something she would stop at just about nothing to get it. Nonetheless, things were still good and life was going well.

* * *

In November of that year I got hired by the Vice President of Atlantic Records to fly over to Kauai to give her surfing lessons. I had done this a year before when she flew me to Waikiki to get her started. Her name was Karen, and she was a strong-minded middle- aged woman who was in good shape and single. She had met this young Hawaiian dude who she had the hots for and he lived on Kauai, so this time we went there instead.

I was stoked, I love Kauai. When we got there a huge swell hit and the surf was great. We were staying in a house she had rented on Hanalei Bay overlooking the beach, a totally cool setup. On about the second day we were there I got up early and went out surfing by myself, figuring I would get in a good session before Karen got up and was ready for lessons.

After being out for quite a while I decided to come in. I took off on a wave and was screaming down the line when it occurred to me that I should straighten out and ride the whitewater to the beach.

The surf was pretty big that day. In that moment where I was thinking about straightening out, unfortunately for me before I did, the lip of the wave came down right on my head.

I was compressed into my board and then churned like a rag doll. I knew right off the bat I was hurt.

It felt like an electric shock in my back, and underwater all I could think of was that maybe I had broken my back. When I finally got to the beach I could not get to my feet and started calling for help.

Where I was and where the people on the beach were sitting was about a block apart. They all thought I was waving at them, and they waved back.

I had to let a swell pick me up so I could get to my feet and start waving for somebody to come down and help me get out of the water. There was no way I could pick up my board or even take off my surf leash.

From here it is kind of a long, and not very fun story of a very painful few days on Kauai before I got a flight home strapped to a backboard most of the way.

I had herniated my L5 disc. My doctor told me that surgery was not the best option and that the best way to treat this was with pain management and a lot of doing nothing. I could lie down and stand up, but it was incredibly painful to try to sit for more than a minute or two. So I loaded up with pain meds and adapted to spending all my time on the couch watching television and waiting for this to heal. Ice cream also became an important pain management tool. And donuts.

Right at this time Jack Flynn decided to close up the surf shop and move his business to San Diego. This was not good; I was laid up and now didn't have a full time job. I was thinking about what to I should do. I had also snapped both of my hernias in the wipe out. I had not known it because the back pain had masked it out and I had not been moving around much. So, I had surgery to repair that and spent a week in the hospital at Hoag in Newport Beach.

Hoag hospital is on a hill and my room had a view where I could see guys taking off on great waves by the Newport Pier, at a place I liked to surf called "Blackies." This was the most pain I was ever in and I was really miserable. After I got home it was back to the couch for more doing nothing. Well, I was doing something. I was gaining weight.

Things were kinda bleak.

* * *

In January my son Tanner Scott Carroll, who I have to say has turned out to be one of the coolest dudes I know, was born.

When Pam had told me she was pregnant with Tanner I was a little shocked because I didn't expect it. She had promised to be on birth control. But Pam was Pam and when she wanted something she would find a way, and she wanted another child.

I was very happy about it though, as I thought it would be cool for Kasey to have a little brother or sister. When he was born I was very happy. A little girl and a little boy, we had a very nice little family.

Tanner and Kasey Carroll decked out in custom wetsuits from Tony Smith at Coral Reef Wetsuits in Fountain Valley, Ca. Photo: Corky

When Jack had told me he was closing the shop my immediate thought was that I would take it over and make it my own. I had mentioned to the owner of the building a couple of times that if Jack ever let go of his lease that I wanted it. So I called him up and told him so again. He said that was fine, and he would get back to me shortly.

I never heard back from him and then found out he had rented it to somebody else. I called him and asked him what the deal was, he blew me off saying, "I didn't really think you were serious." Well, I had been serious and this kinda pissed me off. But, nothing I could do about it.

Around the same time, I heard that Aaron Pai at *Huntington Surf 'n Sport* was adding a "Longboard" section to his shop and let him know that I would be interested in working there if he wanted me.

Then the trifecta of my laid up period came when a local plastic surgeon convinced me that he could remove the huge surf bumps that had grown on my rib cages and that they would never come back. These things had been a concern for a long time and looked very funny, like I had four breasts and the lower ones were pretty big. People were always curious as to what they were but were too embarrassed to ask.

Most thought either I had some horrible tumors or had, in fact, grown breasts. Either way it wasn't good, so they didn't want to ask.

It turned out that my insurance through Screen Actors Guild would cover the surgery, so I went for it. Huge mistake. Not only was the two months of recovery super painful but also the dam things grew back even bigger than they were before once I started surfing regularly again. It was a total waste of time and pain. In later years my kids would tease me and call me "the man with four breasts." The only good part is that it never hurts my ribs when I paddle out, as they are nature's own padding.

The human body is amazing in the lengths it will go to protect itself. Another example of this is "Surfers Ear."

The body will grow little boney bumps in the ear canal to protect the eardrum from cold and wind. These can eventually close the canal and impair your hearing. I have had them removed several times. I finally got with a great doctor who has kept my ears healthy for many years now named Dr. Carol Jackson in Newport Beach.

There are also things that grow on your eyes to protect them from sun glare. Had em, had the surgery. You name it and if it's caused by surfing or sun I have or have had it.

This brings me to the skin cancer issue. We never used sunblock when I was a kid. I started to have problems with skin cancers popping up right about the same time as all this other stuff was going on. A local skin doctor named Sidney Newman started treating me then, and to this day has virtually kept me alive.

More on that later, but just a word of advice thrown in here for good measure: **USE SUNBLOCK!!!**

* * *

So anyway, this was a really difficult stretch of about nine months when I couldn't surf and gained a ton of weight, like 45 pounds. Not good.

But one good thing was that when Aaron opened the longboard part of his shop he hired both me and a good pal of mine named George Lambert to manage that section of the store. At least I had a regular job once again.

I should tell you about George. He is this freckled face big-eyed stoked surf gremmie who was somewhere in his thirties at this time and had been running the tiny Robert August Surf Shop up the street for a number of years.

Robert had recently decided to close it, so both George and I were in the exact same position of looking for a new position.

George is one of those kinds of dudes I like to call a "locals local." He had been raised in Huntington Beach and had gone to Huntington Beach High School just like me.

George was an excellent surfer and had been a big part of the surf team in High School. His dad, also a George, was also a local surfer and very popular.

After High School, young George started working in the surf shop and residing deep in the pack of pier rats that ruled the surfing lineup at the pier. He was a very charismatic kinda guy with a big smile and an even bigger personality. I liked to call him the "Mayor of Main Street." It's funny, but in town, there had been three Georges before him that had big roles in everyday life on Main Street, Surf City, U.S.A.

There had been George Farquhar, who published the local newspaper and was part of the very early crew surfing the pier. The city would name a park after him, after he passed away.

Next there was Little George Patton.

He was called "Little George" because he was, well, little. He opened the infamous Georges Surf Center on the first block of Main Street, just up from the pier. After Little George there was George Draper, who conveniently bought *Georges Surf Center* and therefore didn't need to change the name. Perfect deal.

This George became a fixture on Main Street and was the Mayor of Main Street during his years on the block.

One of the cool things about Georges Surf Center was that it featured one of the very first actual "juice bars" in the back. A beautiful young local surf chick, who for a while dated Mike Doyle, named Jan Gaffney ran it and it was called, you guessed it, "Jan's Juice Bar."

She opened it in the late sixties and has been in business ever since. When *Georges Surf Center* closed up, she moved up the street to her own location.

Working with George at HSS was both a lot of fun and at the same time a totally different "surf shop" kind of experience. I had grown up, as had George, working in surf shops.

Me at *Hobie's* and later *Windansea,* and George at *Robert August's*. We both had surf shop pedigrees, if you will.

We had come from the school where a surf shop was a place where surfboards are sold and business is run on a kinda loose "bro" basis. It's kinda like if Larry is running by, headed to the surf and needs a bar of wax you just toss him one and say, "ride one for me."

HSS was not like that. We wore nametags and punched a time clock. I think that right there explains it all.

We became experts at the art of t-shirt folding. I mean we could make those things as sharp as a military bed. Edges that could cut off a limb. No off color jokes told there, not unless you wanted to be called into the principals' office for a reprimand.

I mention that because that was me. Anybody who knows me will confirm that I love to joke around, which naturally includes telling jokes. It's just part of who I am.

HSS was just a part of the "new" and modern America. Anybody and everybody can and will get offended over just about anything and if you are the perpetrator of the offense it can and will be held against you in a court of law. Or, in this case, Aaron Pai's office.

We had to learn how to exist in a much more "business like" surf shop environment. Now I am not saying that this was wrong or a bad thing. Aaron is a very good and very successful businessman and his way of running a business was probably a much more profitable way to do it. After all, how many actual "surf shops" even exist anymore? Very, very few. If you are gonna run a business then run it business like.

I have nothing but respect for Aaron and that way of thinking. But George and I were kinda surf shop dinosaurs and it took a bit of adaption on our parts to fit into the system. But, with some work, we did, and all was cool.

Then they opened the new *DUKE'S* Restaurant and Bar right across the street, at the base of the pier. Dean Torrance, the *"Dean"* of *Jan and Dean,* recommended me for the job of house musician and they hired me. It was a wonderful gig. I had a tiki bar bandstand on the outside patio that was made by this cool dude named Bamboo Ben.

This was just at the time that I figured out how to have a band without having a band. I love technology, especially music technology.

So let me run this down for you. I had a small home recording studio in my garage. I had a 16-track tape recorder along with a computer based recording system called Digital Performer.

I, like most of the musical world, was in the process of navigating to, and from the world of analog to digital.

Long story short, I could record backing tracks to all my songs. These tracks would have drums, bass, keyboards, pretty much everything I wanted. But they would not have guitar or vocals on them.

I could mix these tracks down to stereo files and load them into a little box that would play them back. I could plug that box into my P.A. system along with my guitar and vocal microphone. Then I could call up whatever song I wanted and hit play. The band was in the box and my guitar and vocals were live.

I still use this same system today, although it has progressed a ton since then, and now I can do way more than just the basic stuff I could do back then. It's cool to be your own band.

CHAPTER 22

"The Distant Sound of Mariachis"

By now the Corky Carroll Surf School was going gangbusters. There was now a branch near Puerta Vallarta, at a little resort called Costa Azul, where I would go for the occasional getaway. Rick Walker was doing very well and had taken a surf trip to Costa Rica and fell in love with it. Soon there was a new Corky Carroll Surf School, more of what you would call a surf camp, down there.

I went down to check it out and had a wonderful time. I liked it too. Rick had a cool two-story house where he could put up the guests and take them surfing at the local beach, which was only about a hundred or so yards away.

While I was there I met a guy named Des Metcalf. Des was successful in the security business in Alabama and had come down to brush up on his surfing skills. He went by the nickname "Blue Dog," and actually reminded me of a big dog. He had a good sense of humor and was very easy going. We hit it off and had a good time hanging out and surfing.

Not long after that, he called me up one day asking if I would take him on a surf trip. He wanted to go somewhere warm and that had good lefts, him being a fellow goofy-foot.

* * *

At this point, let me go back a few months.

I was walking down Main Street in Huntington Beach one morning and saw a painting in the window of a restaurant that had recently closed up and moved to a part of town with more reasonable rent. Main Street was the high rent district.

The painting was of a beautiful wave peeling off with a cantina in the foreground and palm fronded hills in the distance.

My first thought was, "Wow, I wonder where that wave is?"

But the place was closed up so I had no way to find out. I would go by that window every day for a couple of weeks before I found a guy in there. When I asked him where the wave was he said he didn't know but thought it might be someplace in Africa or something. It did not look like Africa to me. When I asked him for the name and phone number of the artist he would not give it to me. He said if I bought the painting he would have the artist contact me. I loved the painting and it turned out to be not all that expensive, so I bought it.

A couple of weeks later a pal of mine named Peter Schworer called me up and said he heard I bought one of his paintings. I had no idea that Peter had done it until he pointed out that his name was on it. Duh! I had not put two and six together I guess.

He invited me over to his house, which was about a mile from mine, and showed me more paintings, and many photos of all these wonderful looking left-hand point breaks in the area near Zihuantanejo on Mainland Mexico. I had spent a lot of time in the past surfing Puerto Escondido and then recently near Puerta Vallarta but had never been to that part of the coast. It looked fantastic and I wanted to go there one day.

***

Okay... This brings me back to the call from Blue Dog. He wants to go somewhere warm that has lefts. Voila!

I immediately think of all those great looking lefts I had seen in Peters paintings and photos and suggest we go to Zihuantanejo. He is all in, and we made plans to meet up down there in a couple of weeks.

Little did I know at that moment that my entire life was on track to make a total change in direction, in the not all that distant future.

We arrive in Mexico and check into a nice Hotel in Ixtapa. This is the resort area just over the hill from Zihuantanejo.

Peter meets us for dinner, (did I mention he lives there most of the time and has an art gallery in Zihuantanejo?)

We make arrangements to hook up in the morning and he is going to show us a very cool spot that would be a good place for Des and me to start out.

Des is on a mission to really get back into surfing and he has the time and resources to do it. My job is to hone his surfing skills and be the driver. He would almost kill us a dozen times on the way from the airport to the hotel on the first day, so it was decided that I was always gonna be the driver.

We show up at a really nice point break called "La Saladita," about thirty or so miles north of town. It is absolutely perfect. Conditions were excellent and the waves were maybe four to six feet. We paddled out and I just fell in love with the place.

It was a really long ride and the water was warm, not to mention it was a virtual tropical paradise. Blue Dog loved it too.

For the next week, we would get up early and drive out to surf there until we were too tired to surf anymore. Then we would go back to the hotel and jump in the pool and have drinks at the swim-up bar. In the evening we would go someplace local to eat and then normally crash early, so we could get up to surf again the next day.

It was a really cool deal. So cool in fact that when the week was over we made arrangements to come back a month later.

This same scenario would play itself out over and over. When there was a good swell running I would take the money that I had made and just stay another week. Why had I never known about this place before? This was much better than getting my brains beat out in the gnarly bone-crushing barrels at Puerto Escondido.

Over the next few years, I would find myself down there more and more, pretty much as often as possible.

* * *

On the home front, things were going along well. Pam was continuing to advance at her job with Tiempo Escrow. She suggested I become a Notary because I could pick up side work doing "mobile document signings." Interest rates had just dropped and there were so many people doing refinancing that they could not keep up with all the appointments to have documents signed. There were just too many clients that didn't have the time to come into the office to do it. As a Notary, I could take the documents to them and witness the signing. In a day, if I planned it right, I could do up to ten signings. The escrow office paid really well for that, and I was able to bring in a ton of extra money. This would work for a few months each time the rates would drop with nothing in-between, but when it was on, it was very profitable.

We had bought ourselves a couple of jet skis and started taking weekend trips out to the Colorado River with the kids. It was really a lot of fun and something we could do together. I always liked those trips. It was something we had in common and it felt good.

Then Des and I found a great deal on a lot in Mexico overlooking the surf break that we had grown to love so much. It was really cheap, for what it was, and we jumped on it within minutes of seeing it. The idea was that we would build a house and then, rather than taking people on surf trips, I could bring them to me instead. I designed a house, and we found a local builder to make it happen.

Corky with cool collage of great memories. Photo: Kasey Carroll

* * *

I am not sure exactly how I should manage the next part of the story, but it is such a huge part of it that I have to tell it. So, I guess the best way is to just tell it.

Pam was always a bit overweight. It never bothered me because her personality was good, and we got along well.

But as time went on and with the birth of the kids, she got bigger. She felt embarrassed about it and many times would not go to functions with me because of it. I always wanted her to come, but she was pretty stubborn when she wanted to be, which was always.

She had done a lot of research on gastric bypass surgery. Brain Wilson's daughter had done it and was a big cheerleader for it. Pam wanted it. I thought it was a really risky deal and tried to convince her to not do it. But, Pam was Pam and she wanted it. End of the conversation.

So, I did my best to support her.

We found a great surgeon in San Diego that was a leader in that field. We went down there and got a hotel room where she could recover after the operation and her time in the hospital. It was important to be as close to the hospital as possible for a couple of weeks after the surgery.

When we finally got home it would be the beginning of a long road to recovery, and a number of follow up surgeries to remove loose skin and reshape her body to the way she wanted to look. It was expensive and a very hard journey on both of us, more her than me naturally, but both of us just the same.

I remember one day asking her, "So... when you get all thin and hot looking are you going to leave me for some hot young dude with a BMW?"

Her reassuring answer was, "How shallow do you think I am? I would never do that!"

Over the next year or so the whole thing developed. She lost all the extra weight and that, combined with a number of jobs with the plastic surgeon, left her looking good.

She got long hair extensions and I have to admit that it was a miraculous transformation in not only the way she looked but also her self-confidence. I was fine with the way she was in the first place but this change made her happy so that was good enough for me.

At the same time, she had been working almost as hard at her job as she had been on the body transformation. She had progressed to being one of the leading escrow officers in Orange County.

She was so dedicated to it that sometimes she would bring me into the office at night after hours to help her with filing and organizing papers for the next day. I was totally behind her, and her quest.

I was very happy doing what I was doing, working at HSS.

My columns, doing music at Dukes, the surf trips to Mexico with Des and landing the occasional T.V. commercial.

With her doing so well in Escrow, I got the idea to start selling real estate. I got my license and a job working for Bob "The Greek" Bolen at Huntington Beach Realty on, yes of course, Main Street.

All of a sudden there was a lot on the plate.

Pam had always wanted a bigger and better house. So, we sold the townhome and bought a really nice three-bedroom home in a cool neighborhood over by where I used to teach tennis at Mile Square Park.

The house had a big garage that I immediately turned into a small home recording studio. We settled in and all was looking good. What looks good on the surface sometimes is just that though.

I'll have to admit that I never saw what was coming next. Never even imagined it. Kind of like the week before the Cat 5 hurricane wipes you out and you had not ever thought it was going to happen to you, but then it does.

I don't want to dwell on this part or go into detail as it is not good and the details are not important. What happened was that when Pam got her new body and was doing so well at her job a part of her came out and took over.

It was the part where she had always been overweight and had never been, in her mind, the hot chick.

She felt like she was always the friend of the hot chick. Now she was the hot chick and she loved it. She wallowed in it. And she just wanted to bask in it and get wild. And she did, big time.

At first, she was pretty stealth and hid it from me well. But then it just got to be so out there and obvious that everybody, including me, knew about it. It wasn't fun at all, well at least for me anyway.

We went to marriage counseling. She said to the counselor that she didn't care about us anymore, she wanted to do what she wanted to do and she was going to continue to do it no matter what.

She did said say that she loved me, but if I wanted to stay married I would have to agree to an open marriage.

The phycologist was kind of shocked, she said she had never encountered anybody so blatant about it before. But it was what it was and I had to figure out how to deal with it.

It all kind of came to a head during a short trip to Cabo San Lucas with a few of our friends. She made it clear to everybody that she wanted to be somewhere else, and with somebody else. It was difficult and made even more so when a hurricane hit. On top of that it was my birthday.

The morning after we got home she said to me, "Why don't you just go to Mexico, you like it there and then I won't have to feel so guilty." She basically was dumping me for a younger dude with a BMW. No, he really had a BMW, no kidding.

This was the final knife to the heart. At that moment I gave up. I also thought about it and realized that this was actually a pretty good idea. Such a good idea, in fact, that I left the next day. The new casa at La Saladita was in the process of being built and I found a little apartment in Ixtapa to live in while the construction was being done.

WHAM!!!

My life changed again, just like that.

CHAPTER 23

"Mexican Time"

Learning to live in Mexico was, well, a "learning" experience. Things happen at a much different pace and in a much different fashion. People that realize that they are the ones who have to adapt, and can do so, are the ones who can successfully make the transition. The Mexicans are not gonna adapt to you and the sooner you get off of the "but that's not the right way to do that" attitude and go with the "oh, so that is the way it's done here" mode, the better off you are gonna be.

When you learn that part you are ahead of the game, many Americans can't do it. But I am not one of them. It would have been easier if I could have spoken a little better Spanish, but I found a way to get by using a lot of hand gestures, sign language and the limited vocabulary that I had from all the time I had spent in Puerto Rico, Puerto Escondido, and Puerta Vallarta.

I had settled into a nice daily routine. I would wake up early, make a cup of coffee and drive out to La Saladita and go surfing.

After surfing, I would go by the construction site on the new casa and check on how the day's progress was going, usually taking cokes, water and snacks to the workers. Then I would maybe surf one more time before heading back to town. At that time, I would swim in the pool and then take a nap.

I got a job playing music at night at a very cool cantina bar on the side of the mountain overlooking Zihuantanejo Bay, called Casa Bahia.

I worked four nights a week and part of my deal with them was that I could eat and drink for free anytime I wanted. So, needless to say, I would eat there every night.

It was one of the most fun gigs I ever had. The view over the bay was amazing and the cool evening breeze was just perfect.

As I was pretty much the only "gringo music" in town, I had a good following and always did well in tips. Plus the fact that my hours were from 7 pm to 10 pm, I was able to get to bed early enough to make it easy to get up at dawn and drive out to surf dawn patrol for those sweet La Salidita lefts. All in all, it was a pretty sweet set up.

To go with the gig at Casa Bahia, I was able to bring a few of my surfing clients down and set them up at the Krystal Hotel. I would take them surfing every day at La Saladita. It was coming together about as well as I could have hoped under the circumstances.

Somewhere along the way I met a nice looking Chica. Her name was Karla, and she lived in Morelia, which is about 4 hours from Ixtapa. We went out a few times when she would come down for the weekend with her friends, it was a nice little budding romance. Plus, she did a good job of taking the sting out of the marriage breakup.

It took a total of seven months from groundbreaking to moving into the new casa, and I had been there for five of them.

***

My lifelong pal, Tim Dorsey's house was being built at the same time, a few lots away. On the day the Electric Company flipped the switch and turned on the power, we both moved into our new casas. I will never forget that day.

Me, being a dedicated television addict, had made arrangements with a local dude, who sold bootleg satellite T.V. set ups, to set me up on that day. They tuned the power on at 10 A.M.

I moved in around noon. The T.V. guy was there at 3 and had me set up by 5. Tim and I had dinner on my deck, followed by more than one celebratory drink. At 9am, I was in bed, in the new casa, in a tropical paradise with a perfect left-hand point break out the window and watching the best television set up I ever had. The bootleg box gave me Dish Network from the U.S., including everything they had in the way of programming in all 4 time zones.

I thought to myself, "Well, here I am. I think this will be my last stop." The only thing was that I was alone. I missed my kids a lot and never really did "alone" all that well either. But that was probably a good thing for me just then. I needed a "reboot," and this was just that. A whole new life was in front of me.

CHAPTER 24

"Corkarita Time"

Sinking into my new life at La Saladita was not all that hard.

Yes, it was a constant learning experience as to how to maintain a house right on the beach and to survive the tropics at the same time, not to mention get my footing as a single man again.

Tim's wife had moved down with him but bailed on him very quickly once they moved into the La Saladita casa, not liking life pretty far from normal civilization.

So we were both on our own, and spent a lot of time hanging out together, like almost every night, on my deck swapping stories that we had told each other tons of times but still seemed to enjoy doing.

We had known each other for so long and had both grown up in the Seal Beach / Huntington Beach surf scene, that it seemed like we had endless stories of things in common from our past. These would get rehashed over and over and it never got old.

Tim has a real gift of gab, like the dude can talk your ears off very easily. And, as a little side benefit to our evening chats, I started working on inventing new and better "cocktails" for the dailysunset.

There was, of course, the "Saladita Sunset," which was a favorite until I came up with my now infamous signature drink, the "Corkarita." It's like a Margarita but much better, at least in my totally unbiased opinion.

Corky and Tim "The Iguana" Dorsey. Mexico. Photo: Raquel Sauza Carroll.

Cocktail experimenting with Timoteo was/is always a never ending adventure.

Like the night that we got all set up to barbeque some steaks on the deck while I was working on how to make "dirty" martinis. A storm came in and lightning started striking all over the place. A huge bolt hit a palm tree about thirty feet away from us and blew the top right off of it.

After a very short discussion, it was decided it might be a good idea, and safer, if we took the barbeque, and ourselves out to the other side of the house, away from the beach and out of the wind.

Between sunset and around 2am, the two of us consumed a bottle and a half of Stoli's (Vodka) and had, for some unknown reasonthat neither of us remembers, smoked an entire pack of Camel cigarettes that somebody had left in the house. And, too add, I have really never smoked. Tim chews cigars but rarely ever lights one up. Why we thought it might be cool to light up the Camels is still a mystery.

Plus, during the course of the evening's martini sampling and Camel smoking, Tim peed into my new barbeque. Good thing it was after we had eaten our steaks. I saw him walk over towards it but didn't know why.

Then I say him start to pull out "tiny Tim" and tried to yell "Nooooooooo, NOT in the barbecue." But, too late.

Of course, he was peeing directly into the wind and probably more got on him than in the barbecue, but I had to throw it away anyway. My stomach hurt from laughing. NOT as bad as my head did the next morning though.

I remember paddling out to surf wondering which had done more damage, the vodka or the Camels. Either way it was one of those, "okay, not a good idea to repeat THAT night" kinda things.

But, truth be told, we don't always learn from our mistakes the first time. Or the second. Or, so on and so on.

There was also the night that I saved Tim's life.

We had been sitting on the deck having drinks and chit chatting as usual. At 9:30 I went to bed to watch the LAKERS game on TV. The time difference is 2 hours, so the 7:30 start times in Los Angeles are actually 9:30 down here. Tim headed home.

At halftime of the game, I would normally walk out on the balcony and check the yard and beach with a very high-powered flashlight that I had at the time. There was a little path that led between his house and mine and in the middle was a barbed wire fence that we would stretch the wires to go through when going back and forth.

As I shined the light, I saw that Tim was stuck in the fence and hanging by his T-Shirt.

He looked just like that dude who was dead and stuck on a tree in the river at the end of the movie "Deliverance." His arm was up over his head and the whole deal. The entire upper part of his body was in the air, but his lower half was laying on the ground. I yelled down to him, "Hey Timoteo, is that you?"

"Uh, uh huh, yeah."

"Are you stuck in the fence?"

"Uh, uh huh, think so." Did I mention he/we had drank a lot that night?

"You need some help?" "Uh, uh huh, yeah."

"OK, I will be down after the game, hang on." "Uh, uh huh." Naturally, I went right down to help him.

When I got there I noticed that his legs were all black. At first, I thought he was just dirty; he has a habit of that.

However, upon closer investigation, I saw that his whole lower half was completely covered with red ants.

They were eating him. Eating him alive, at that. Yikes.

So, I got him out of the fence and to his house where I sprayed him down with the hose until all the ants were gone.

The next morning we could see that they had eaten off all of the skin on his legs, they were raw and red and gooey looking. Yuck.

If I had not seen him they would have eaten him totally up. There would have been nothing left but bones and a pair of really rank Speedos that NOTHING would dare eat. I saved the dude's life.

Obviously living next to Tim has been an adventure.

* * *

One of my favorite stories to tell about him is the story of the "Frozen Dog." This has become a bit of local folklore around here.

The best part is, it's all true. Even though you will doubt me when I tell it. There is nothing made up or even slightly embellished about this tale, whatsoever!

It all started when we first moved into our houses.

Tim's wife, who had six dogs, was still with him at the time. Her dogs were not at all popular in the neighborhood. They would bark at everybody and try to bite them. She walked them on six leashes and wherever she went it was a total barkathon, with a lot of snarling and snapping thrown in.

The worse part was that a few times they actually did bite some people. Tim was always having to pay for their treatment or lost wages if they couldn't work.

These were bad doggies.

Everybody was mad at them all the time, and people threatened her that if they bit them, that they would kill them.

Even me, I told her if any of them ever bit me I would shoot it.

Of course, this was an idle threat because, for one thing, I didn't own a gun at that time and the fact that I am such a dog lover that I never could do that, no matter how mad at it I was.

At this moment, as I am writing this some years later, we have six dogs and a cat, so that kinda clues you in to how much I love dogs.

Anyway, the point being that nobody liked her dogs and many people had warned her.

Then one morning she woke up and found one of her dogs was dead.

She totally freaked out and was sure somebody had killed it, even though there were no marks on it or gunshot holes, machete hacks, or anything at all. It was just dead.

She rousted Timoteo and screamed at him to get up and that they were going to take the dead dog to town to the vet to get an autopsy. I don't remember the exact name of the dog, but I think it was "Muffy." So, we are gonna go with that.

"Autopsy? Are you nuts, it's a dog!" He replied through red bloodshot eyes and a throbbing gin induced headache.

He could have saved himself some grief and just gone along with it as he was NEVER going to win this debate in a million years.

(As a side note) In this relationship Mrs. Timoteo was the boss, by far and away. A dictator if you will, of the highest order.

The Fidel Castro of wives!

"She said, GET UP!!! We are going to get an autopsy and find out how poor Muffy was murdered."

No, not simply killed, it was MURDERED, she yelled!!! "Yes dear" ol' Timoteo replied, in his nicest caring voice. He should have just led with that in the first place.

Of all the words he ever spoke to her these were the only two that had any effect on her one way or another.

If he stuck to these he was okay, any deviation at all and it would turn into a horrible shriek fest.

I've heard it way too many times myself, so I can imagine poor Timoteo, lord knows he had a mountain of them on top of him daily. It was not pretty.

So, off they go to Ixtapa to see the vet and get an autopsy on the dog.

When they get there and Tim tells Dr. Jorge (the vet) what they would like him to do, he first opened his eyes really wide, then broke out in a big laugh. "Autopsy? Are you kidding, they barely do those on people down here Tim!

Dr. Jorge adamantly points out... THIS is A DOG."

At which point the wife defiantly shrieked "I WANT AN AUTOPSY DONE AND I WANT IT DONE NOW!!!!!"

I don't think she was gonna take no for an answer.

Dr. Jorge kinda did a double take, thought about it for a few moments, and replied, "O.K., I can do that, but it will cost 500 U$ Dollars."

Tim, at least a little hopeful this would put an end to it, looked over at the wife and said, "Honey, we can't afford that much money."

To which she once again even more defiantly shrieked, "I SAID, I WANT AN AUTOPSY DONE AND I WANT IT DONE NOW."

She obviously figured that somebody had killed Muffy, and she wanted proof. Now, I am not sure what she planned to do about it, but I am sure it wasn't gonna be good, and am even more sure it wasn't gonna be any fun for Tim.

So, Tim agrees to the deal and Dr. Jorge takes the dead dog into the back room to perform the doggietopsy.

Wife and Tim sit in the lobby not speaking a word while this happens. This was one of those times when thirty minutes seems like all day, and poor Tim was just wishing he was anywhere else but there.

Finally, Dr. Jorge returns from the back room, a few blood smears on his apron and a fairly blank look on his face. He matter of factly reports, "Well, it's a dog. And it's dead. Natural causes." And then after a brief pause, "That will be 500 U$ Dollars."

Unfortunately, he didn't close the door to the back room very well and the breeze kinda blew it open. Just enough for el wifo to see the dead Muffy's head on a tray.

At that moment she went screaming out to the car in semi hysteria. I have no idea what the conversation between Tim and Dr. Jorge went like. But I suspect there was some sort of mention that it was a shame that it had to be, the dog.

A few minutes later Tim returned to the car and reassuringly tells the wife that he paid for the autopsy and that Dr. Jorge would take care of disposing of the body, thinking this would satisfy the totally ballistic she-beast that he had married. But nooooo.

"WHAT? Oh no he is not. She is a family member and we need to bury her, go get her right now."

Resigning himself to the reality that this thing is not going to be over until it was over, he went back in and got the remains of the dog in a plastic bag and put it in the car.

They drove home in dark silence.

When they got home Tim, once again attempting, and once again unsuccessful, to be reassuring said, "I will go dig her a nice grave under the palm tree by the beach." Wrongly thinking that this would please her, and just hoping for some sort of peace.

But Nooooo.

"WHAT? Are you freaking crazy you stupid idiot? She is a family member, we can't bury her without a ceremony. And I have to send off to Japan to get a burial gong for that. You can't bury her until that happens, don't you know ANYTHING????"

"Yesss Dear. But what should I do with Muffy until then?"

"Put her in the freezer, obviously. Why are you sooooo flat out STUPID?"

"Yesss Dear."

With that, Tim calmly cleared out the freezer on the top of their kitchen refrigerator and placed the plastic bag with the dog corpse inside. To be preserved, until the said burial gong made its way to Mexico from Japan.

Just the mention of "to Mexico from Japan" should give you some sort of idea of how long this was gonna take.

A couple of weeks after this happened the wife decides she doesn't want to live at La Saladita anymore.

Personally, I think she felt that nobody liked her. She was still positive that the ultimate evil had been done to poor little Muffy. In any case she packed up and moved out, leaving Tim alone and expecting him to protect that refrigerator with his life.

* * *

During the first year we lived out here, there were frequent power outages. Any little thing, a breeze, a bird landing on the wire, a drop of rain or a loud fart and the power would go out.

Such was the case one day when Tim had gone to town with a long list of things that the wife needed him to do for her. It wasn't until about eight o'clock that night that he showed up at my house for dinner and drinks, and he had been gone since seven that morning.

After eating and while sitting on the deck having cocktails and chit- chatting for a while I mentioned to him that the power had been off all day and had just come back on only a few minutes before he got there. Now, this wasn't all that uncommon at that time he didn't think all that much about it, at first.

A little bit later all of a sudden he lets out, "OH SHIT, the dog." Not knowing what he is talking about I go, "huh?"

To which he explains that his old refrigerator is one that has to be "reset" anytime you turn it off or it loses power, so for all he knows poor Muffy has been thawing out all day.

This is the tropics and temperatures during the day are almost always in the 90s. But, after fretting about it for a few minutes, and a few more sips on his drink, he relaxes and accepts the fact that there is nothing he can do about it at the moment, that he can't do in a little while when he goes home.

So, we go back to chit-chatting, laughing and consuming whatever tasty beverage it was that we were consuming that evening.

Normally it would be him drinking red wine and me some sort of tequila concoction that I had mixed up, the same careful research and experimentation in this area that would eventually give birth to the aforementioned and now world famous *"Corkarita."*

After many more stories told and cocktails consumed Tim would make his way home and immediately hit the bed and fall asleep.

The next morning the surf was good, and we had a great session together.

I always loved surfing with Tim, he is loud and bellows all sorts of crazy things. He will take off on a wave and declare to all with earshot, "Blubber in motion stays in motion, so look out."

It's always a joyful experience being out there with Tim.

Later that evening he came over for dinner and drinks. By the way, this dinner and drinks thing at my house is a daily thing with us, and after eating we were kicked back in our usual deck chairs, on the deck, and of course, chit-chatting and having more drinks.

Sometime during the evening I casually inquired if the frozen Muffy had melted the day before... or not?

"OH SHIT!!!! The Fridge!"

Yep, he had forgotten all about ole Muffy Dog, and had not done the required re-set. Ooops!

Now we are two full days of meltage, and Tim is not feeling good about this at all. But, after a few minutes of grave concern, he figures that there is nothing he can do about it that he can't when he returns home a little later. So, we go back to chit-chatting, laughing and happily consuming cocktails.

It's not until late the next afternoon when he is thinking about a snack and goes to the fridge to grab a tomato that he remembers that the fridge is off. NOW he does NOT wanna open it.

He does NOT want to see what has become of the formerly frozen Muffy.

So, he resets the thing and totally wraps it up in bubble wrap and duct tape. He will deal with it at a later date and doesn't want it to stink up the house in the event that it starts to smell bad.

This, at least for now, will solve that problem.

Of course, he doesn't have a fridge to use now, but oh well, who needs a fridge all that bad anyways. The pioneers didn't need fridges so why should he.

Over the course of the next year or so there were many more power outages and many more times that Tim forgot to reset the bubble wrapped box. Just part of the way it went.

Then one day ol' Timo needed to go back to California for a couple of weeks.

He enlisted this dude who went by the name "Pulpo" to stay in his house and look after things.

By now Tim had a couple of living dogs and they would need to be fed.

Pulpo was a white dude with long blonde dreadlocks who normally lived in his van.

He liked staying at Tim's place and invited a bunch of his pals and other assorted passersby to stay there too.

There were parties going on pretty much every night over there. One night I wandered over just to see if the house was okay.

When I got there Pulpo and some other crazy looking dude happily informed me that they had decided that the "frozen dog" needed to be buried and finally put to rest.

And, seeing as how nobody wanted to unwrap and open the fridge, they were going to bury the whole thing the next day. As there was a whole pack of them and it seemed like there was nothing I could say to change their mind on this.

I went back home and wondered how Tim was gonna handle this when he got back home.

But this was May. And in May it hasn't rained for months and months, summer is the rainy season here and in winter it is dry as a bone. The ground was like iron and there was no way any of these stoners were gonna get a shovel into the dirt.

So, the plan was off. But, not completely.

The next night one of them shows up at my house and tells me that due to the failure at the day's burial attempt, they had changed directions. Now the plan was to bury the fridge at sea. They wanted to borrow a bunch of my boards, so they could float it out past the shorebreak in front of Tim's house and drop in into the ocean just offshore. This was going to form a reef that would be good for the local sea life, as well as possibly form a new surfing spot.

Dam, this is not all that bad an idea, I was thinking. I even had a name for the newly formed surf spot, we would call it "Dead Dog Reef." Yep, I was down for it.

The next morning we got six of my biggest boards over there and were ready to float'er out there.

When they turned over the fridge it was so heavy that five of them together could not pick it up.

So, they put it back up and gave up on that great idea.

And, of course, in typical stoner fashion, they neglected to plug it back in or reset it.

It wasn't until long after Tim got home and noticed that it was not plugged in that he asked me if I knew anything about it. Pretending to not know anything about it I went, "huh?"

Not too long after that is when Tim got the call one morning from the wife that her cat had died.

Of course, this meant that she wanted, well more like demanded, that Tim go pick it up and stick it in the freezer along with the now many times frozen Muffy.

So he went to town and picked up the lifeless kitty and drove it back out to the house, all the while dreading that he was going to finally have to unbubblewrap the fridge and discover what had transpired over all this time.

This was not what he wanted to do at all. But there was no getting out of it, so when he got home he bravely opened it up.

Inside the fridge itself there was stuff growing on the walls that can only be described as "chia" tomatoes. Hairy stuff that had once been actual tomatoes.

I don't even want to get into the remains of all the milk that had been spilled when Pulpo and the gang had laid the thing on the ground. In short, it was REALLY gross. And, naturally, ol' Timoteo had to deal with the freezer.

The frozen and unfrozen dog parts had come out of the bag and mixed with all the frost built up and what remained was something sort of like "dogcicles" stuck to the walls, roof and bottom.

Poor Tim had no choice but, to scrape it all off and let it thaw out, so he could return what was left to the plastic bag. Once all that was done he took a hose and cleaned out the entire thing, put the cat in its own plastic bag and placed it inside the freezer along with Muffy.

He also went back to using the refrigerator.

It was a couple of weeks after that when I was over at his house one day and I saw that the fridge was not still bubble wrapped and asked him about it. He told me about the cat and the whole sordid mess of cleaning it out.

As I had never seen any frozen pets before, I wondered how they both fit. I just had to go over and open the freezer to see how he had packed them in there.

At first I did a double take; I was not sure I was actually seeing what I was actually seeing. Then I had to ask Tim, "Hey Tim, are SURE that this cat was dead before he stuck it in here?"

He innocently said, "Yeah, why?"

I informed him that he might want to come check it out.

Somehow the dead, or more than likely not so dead, cat had clawed its way halfway out of the bag. It's head and one claw were sticking out and it looked like it had frozen to death in some sort of horrible death scream. Really freaky looking.

When poor Tim saw it he went berserk. "OH NOOOO!!!, OH NOOOOOOO!!!! OH GOD, OH GOD OH GOD NOOOOO!!!!"

Now, let me say that Tim is a real animal lover, and this just totally spun him out. His heart was beating right out of his chest, kinda like in a cartoon, and he was pacing back and forth across the room in complete panic mode. I was worried he was gonna blow a main right then and there.

"Don't tell my wife, don't tell my wife. OH GOD, OH NOOOOOO!!!"

It took me a long time to calm him down and assure him that his wife never needs find out about this little error.

Although, in reality, it was her fault. She was the one who had pronounced it dead.

Must have just been sick or passed out or something, Tim never saw it move or do anything to suggest it was still alive, even when he was putting it into the plastic bag. But still, best that she does not find out about the final death of the cat.

I think this scared Tim for life. It's a good thing he was already old.

Then finally, after a few years had gone by, she received the long- awaited burial gong from Japan. She called Tim and said it was time for the burial.

Upon hearing this happy news he said he would dig the graves under the palm tree by the beach for Muffy and the Kitty.

But nooooo. She wanted to bury them in her backyard in Ixtapa.

So, Tim would need to load up his pick-up truck with the two corpses along with all of his animals, as they were all family members and had to be on hand for the ceremony with the gong.

At that time Tim had a goat (more on her to come), four dogs, a cat and a turtle.

He loaded them all into the cab of his NOT extended cab truck and headed down the highway to town, the dead members in two ice chests in the back.

Now, to give you a visualization on this scene, Timoteo had the windows partly down so the goat, and a couple of the dogs could stick their heads out and was wearing his normal get up.

His usual attire of a really dirty and stained white t-shirt, really dirty, smelly and stained blue speedos, and his old straw had that had a bicycle squeeze horn on it along with two red reflectors.

He used the squeeze horn to call the dogs and the goat when they would take walks on the beach and somebody would fall behind.

This was usually the goat who seemed to delight in peeing on unsuspecting people laying on beach towels or eating their purses when they were not looking. A bad goat.

So anyway, there they are rolling down highway 200 heading Ixtapa way, in all their glory when they come upon a military check point.

These check points would consist of a number of heavily armed military guys who all looked about sixteen years old.

They would glare at you and ask where you are coming from and where you were going, all the while giving you the idea that if your answers were not good things were gonna get bad.

They could have just asked if you had any guns or drugs, but they didn't.

Every now and then they would want to search your car.

On this particular day, when this really crazy looking old gringo came rolling up with a truck full of dogs, a cat, a turtle, and a goat.

The Federales felt the need to find out what was going on here. So they ordered him out of the truck, at the same time noticing the ice chests in the back.

Normally a gringo with ice chests means either cold water or a cold beer. And they like both of those things, so we're eager to see what treasures await inside.

When they opened them up and found a dead cat in one, and parts of a dead dog in the other, things got dark and fast.

They immediately drew down on Tim with their AK-47s aimed right at his chest.

He was standing there with his hands in the air just trembling in his horrible stained t-shirt, rancid Speedos and with the hat with the horn and red reflectors on it.

These guys were totally disgusted that this wacko mother was eating his family pets.

In fact, they thought, he could be selling them to the Oriental restaurant in Zihuantanejo that had been long suspected of serving dog and cat. In any case, they were not happy about this and looked like they were gonna shot him at any moment.

Timoteo at that point, said that he was so scared that he even peed a little bit in his Speedos. I am sure that this was not the first time for that though, so this was no big revelation.

The head military dude called this into headquarters while the rest of the squad kept their guns squarely on Tim. This took about twenty minutes in the blazing hot sun. Nobody was happy and the tension was very, very, very, high.

It turns out that it is not against the law to transport dead animals in ice chests and there is nothing they can hold Tim on. They had to let him go, but they don't want to and were really pissed off about it.

They all spit on him and kicked dirt on him and rudely slammed him back into his truck. As he rolled away he gave them a little honk on his hat squeeze horn, to which they all flipped him off.

Later that day Muffy and the kitty were at last laid to rest in the wife's backyard to a few words and the bong of the burial gong.

Which I might add, was the exact same gong I had received many years before when the Funk Dog Surf Band had won the Gong Show on television.

CHAPTER 25

"A Learning Rebound"

As I was getting set up and finding my comfort zone living in the new casa at La Saladita, things started to heat up with the romance I was having with Karla, the girl I told you about who lived in Morelia.

It was at this point that things sort of went crazy on many fronts and the vision I had for the next few years took a drastic turn to the left.

As has been with a couple other not fun parts of this story, I don't want to dwell on this a whole lot because as I look back on it now, I just have to consider it a good, and not so good, in some ways learning experience.

So, I am gonna make this part as brief as I can, but it is an important part of the story.

Karla and I had been seeing much more of each other and things had become a bit hotter and heavier.

Then, Pam decided that she didn't want to have to take care of the kids for a while and told me that I needed to go back to California for the summer, so she could "have a break."

Summer at La Saladita would be slow for any kind of business and I could probably play music at Duke's and maybe work a little, giving private lessons at the surf school. So I agreed to return for the summer, and that I would stay in the house with the kids while she did whatever it was she wanted to do.

This sounded ok on paper but, turned out very different.

I asked Karla if she wanted to ride up to California with me, and that she could fly back as soon as she needed to, while I stayed for the summer.

Somewhere along the journey, in Mazatlán I think it was, we went out and had dinner and a lot of drinks. We were great party partners at that time, which probably was due to the fact that we would only see each other for a night or two at a time, and those usually would consist of going out, drinking and partying.

Somewhere during this particular night, we got engaged.

On this seemingly high note, and unbeknownst to me at the time, this was sort of the turning point when things started to go south, while we were heading north.

When we got back to California, I found a huge stack of unpaid bills, and the kids waiting for me.

Along with divorce papers and a note from Pam that said, "good luck, I am done with all this."

The bottom line was she was not coming back after summer and she expected me, with no money, to pay all these bills and to take care of the kids from that point on.

As you can imagine, I was in a state of shock.

I called her and asked how she expected me to do this, and her honest to goodness reply was "They are hiring at Burger King." Who was this woman?

Anyway, in my attempt to make this part as short as possible. We got divorced, Karla moved up to California with her two kids, and moved in with me, and my two kids. Shortly after, we got married and tried to figure out how we were going to live.

My partner Des had been talking about wanting to open a surf shop in Panama City, near where he lived in Dothan, Alabama.

He offered me a very good deal to move back there, which included using my name on the shop, and for me to manage it 5 months out of the year. The other 7 months I could be back in Mexico doing my surf adventure packages.

This seemed to be a good solution, so I went for it.

We sold the house in California, giving half to Pam, and moved to Alabama to work in the surf shop and set up a home there.

Shortly after getting all set up with a nice house, and the kids in school, and all that necessary stuff. Des informed me that he actually didn't have the money to do the surf shop after all.

Now, this is AFTER I bought a house and got all set up. Yikes, things were not good.

Karla and my daughter did not get along at all, it was a constant war, with me in the middle.

I put the house back up for sale and the plan was to get back to Mexico and get the surf adventure business going stronger, as soon as possible.

It was in March when Des told me no surf shop, September when the house sold, and I was able to go back south.

In the middle of all that Karla went bonkers over some seemingly harmless mischief with the kids and left to go back to Morelia, where she was from. It was not clear what our future, if there was one, was at that time.

Over the next few weeks, she decided she wanted to open a spa and live in Morelia with her kids in school there.

We would stay married and rent a place in Morelia. I would commute as often as I could, and she would come down to the beach every other weekend, or when she could.

After the house in Alabama sold I got back home to La Saladita and the plan was set in motion.

Long distance romance is hard. Long distance marriage is just plain stupid.

* * *

By the next summer, things were not going well, and we split up, only to make the mistake of getting back together in the fall. We tried to make it work for the next year, but it really seemed like we were great daters but not good marriage partners.

It blew up! A quick divorce ensued, and back to square one as far as relationships went.

But, not exactly square one really.

* * *

During the three or four months that Karla and I had been split up the year before, I had met and dated a wonderful girl name Raquel Sauza, who had just moved to Zihuantanejo from Mexico City with her mother.

Raquel was great, and we had nice times together, but it just had not blossomed to the point where we really had a true lasting relationship, yet. It was just going out to dinner and that was totally it.

That for the time being slipped away, and I got back with Karla, which didn't last.

But, as fate would bless me, a few days after Karla and I broke up. I ran into Raquel in the market.

We talked (I sweet talked) and made a date to meet for a coffee. That coffee date actually turned out to be a dinner, then another, then another, and then things seemed to really take on a new and different vibe.

It was like the first time we went out, neither of us was really ready for the other, but some way, somehow we knew, we both were.

She sent me a text asking if I wanted to be her "novio" again.

So, we agreed to meet again, and had a great dinner at our favorite restaurant in town, Banditos, and talked it all out.

I said to Raquel that I did not want to have any more kids and she told me she did not want to have kids at all.

So that being agreed to, and everything else really going perfectly, we committed to each other to give it a shot.

BEST DECISION EVER!!!

Corky and Raquel on their deck, La Saladita, Mexico.

***

The courtship of Raquel was in all meaning of the word, TRADITIONAL.

It was almost a quest in many ways.

We dated and fell in love and dated and kissed a little bit and dated some more.

But she never came home with me. Finally, after months of dating and kissing and being in love, she agreed in coming to the casa. I was very happy about this too, as you might imagine.

So, the big night arrives and I picked her up from work. When she asks if we can stop at her house to pick up her stuff.

I say sure and we go over there, she runs in the house and comes back out with her mom, her brother, her brothers girlfriend, another friend and the family dog, Pepe.

She says everybody is hungry and asks if we can go eat before heading out to La Saladita.

O.K. sure, dinner would be good.

Then after eating I was driving back to her house to drop everybody off when she asks me where we are going.

I replied, "to drop everybody off."

To which she laughs and says that the whole crew is coming with us.

Well, obviously that night did not go at all the way I had thought it would.

This was really a project and took a lot of patience on my part. In the long run it was all well worth it.

Raquel is far more than well worth the wait, and I am very glad I did.

On Christmas Eve 2007, she moved in with me.

CHAPTER 26

"Finally Happy and Out to Pasture… Where I Belong!!!"

It's now summer of 2008. Raquel had been living with me for about 6 months and things were really good between us. We got married on July 31, the day my divorce from Karla was final.

Which was ironic because I married Karla on the day my divorce from Pam was final.

I wasn't a single man for more than a few hours over the course of three marriages.

I would think that I was really stupid, and maybe I was the first time, but seeing as how things have worked out so well with Raquel, I am sure that I did EXACTLY the right thing.

A lot has happened over the past eleven years, and while a lot is exactly the same. Life is, oh' so much better now that I truly have the bride of my dreams, here in our little slice of paradise!

It is now 2019 as I am coming to the end of this part of my story.

Together we have built up the surf adventure business and made a really good life for ourselves.

She has fallen in love with living out here in this tropical surf wilderness, something not many city girls would have done. Our relationship has gone from great, to some word that means far more than great, or amazing, or any other adjective I know to describe how good it is.

We really connect on all levels and at last I can honestly say, I am totally, truly happy with my life, thanks to my wife...

I love you baby!!!

EPILOGUE

I started playing music again somewhere along the line, performing small concerts at local hotels and restaurants, and upon special request, I will still perform at venues across the globe.

This led to writing some new songs and that brought forth getting a record deal a few years ago with a fantastic independent label named DARLA Records.

They have re-released most of my older albums, put out a *"Best of Corky Carroll"* album and then a new album titled *"Blue Mango."*

This album was recorded mostly in California with a fantastic line up of musicians. We have Chris Darrow, Richard Stekol, Brad Fiedel, Matt Magiera, Matt Marshall and Doug Miller.

These guys are all well-known and have worked with some of the biggest names in music. We named the band the *"Piranha."*

Plans are now underway for a second album as soon as I write enough new material. So, the music part of my life is in a perfect place. I perform about once a month, which is ideal, as that way it's fun and not work.

Along with the music I also still write two weekly columns for the Orange County Register in Southern California. Thank goodness for email.

Corky's BLUE MANGO album on DARLA records.
Artwork by Marc Jackson of Gold Rush Tattoos, Newport Beach, CA.

I have also reconnected with HOBIE surfboards recently. Releasing the Corky Carroll designed Stand Up Paddleboards and re-issuing a few of my old models from the 1960s.

Plus I have some products on the market online under Corky Carroll Surf Company and am just starting a new company, along with my pal Joel Saltzman, called Blue Mango Surf.

Concert poster 2018. Graphic layout by William Mertz.

On top of all that I sell a little real estate here and there, which really comes in handy when it happens. And, just to fill another little urge I have, I do the occasional painting and manage to even sell a few now and then.

My kids and grandson are all doing well.

Clint has grown into an amazing person and continues to grow and branch out. My grandson Cannon works with him at Clint Carroll's Surf School.

Tanner is great and doing flooring, amazingly cool for a Carroll kid.

Kasey graduated from UCSB with straight A's.

I love them all.

* * *

I surf most every day, and we have Tim over for dinner most every night.

We have taken it as our mission to take care of him and make sure he is fed and well groomed, but that last part is, well, impossible.

The dude has been deep… Way TOO long!!!

A lifetime of chewing cigars, with the past 16 years of little to no personal hygiene have taken a toll on his daily, well, scent. It has a life of its own. Sometimes we make him jump into the neighbor's pool before letting him into the house. Not our pool, heck no.

But damn, we love him!!!

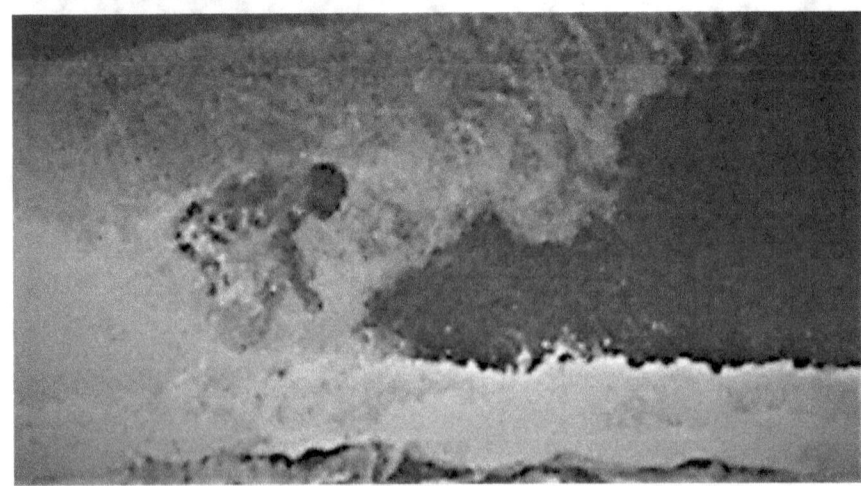

Corky surfing at his home break of La Saladita, Mexico.
Photo: Raquel Sauza Carroll, FINS DOWN SURF PHOTOS.

Raquel and Venus Carroll. Photo: Corky

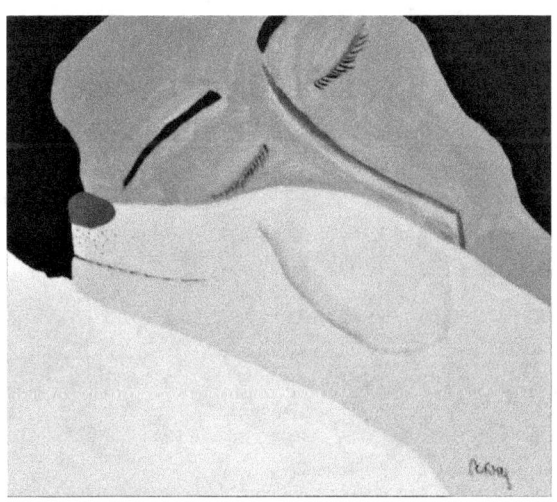

"GIRL/DOG" - Painting by Corky

My Beautiful Daughter - Kasey

Carroll boys: Clint, Corky, Cannon (grandson) and Tanner.
Photo: Raquel Sauza Carroll

Inducted to both the International Surfing Walk
of Fame and the Surfers Hall of Fame

Corky heading down for his daily therapy session at his home break
- La Salidita, Mexico

Corky's Artwork. Photo: Duke Parker

Corkarita time... Another Beautiful Sunset in Paraiso!!!
Photo: Duke Parker

EPILOGUE II

How can I describe Raquel to you?

She is beautiful inside and out, and her sense of humor fits perfectly with mine. We are both a little twisted when it comes to seeing the humor in things, works out nice like that. We will both see something and crack up at the same time. Others might not find that particular thing funny, but we do.

And she gives me no slack at all. If I mess up, she makes sure I know about it and won't let it happen again, and she bites.

Bites Hard!!!

She is very good at running a husband and takes excellent care of me. In turn I try as hard as I can to spoil her rotten and have done an amazing job at it. She is truly one of a kind... and thankfully mine!

But, I think that the most important part is we just have fun together all the time, we love being with each other. That is so important.

When we are not together we miss each other a lot.

On top of all of this, Raquel is an amazing cook and makes dinner for our guests each night, this really adds to the ambiance of the surf package. Plus, she is a fantastic dancer, she loves to dance more than about anything that I can think of.

She recently discovered ZUMBA and jumped in full bore.

Over the past couple of years Raquel has gotten certified as an instructor in just about every kinda of Zumba that there is. Including Aqua Zumba, Easy Zumba, Strong Zumba, Zumba for Dummies and about any other kind of Zumba known to man or beast. She even does Zumba for Doggies with our pack each morning, its dog gone crazy.

Did I mention we have, at the moment, 6 dogs and a cat?

Well we do. Our room is more kennel than bedroom, but we love it that way.

When I am laying on our bed, in "my spot," and Raquel is next to me and all the doggies are spread out all over us, I am at peace with the world and as content as a clam at high tide. It just does not get any better than this.

I am so lucky, and most grateful to have had this long and crazy life. For surfing, and music, and many fantastic friends, my kids, loves known and loves lost, and best of all winding up in this incredibly beautiful place where we live, and to be with the girl of my dreams, living the life of my dreams.

I can't really tell you the rest...
Because we're...

Not Done Yet!

If you'd like to join in on the fun, sun and great surf... Raquel and I cordially invite you to down to our little slice of paradise, and to help us create the next chapter.
Email me at corkysurf@aol.com for info.

If you enjoyed the book, and are so inclined, a review would be most appreciated. (email below)

Should you be interested in distribution, bulk purchases or would like to utilize any portion of the content for promotional or educational purposes. Contact Duke Parker at TheProductivityGroup@gmail.com

www.ingramcontent.com/pod-product-compliance
Lightning Source LLC
Chambersburg PA
CBHW071350290426
44108CB00014B/1493